FRUITFUL BUSINESS

To Marjan

May your business
endeavours be fruitful

All the best for 2013

FRUITFUL BUSINESS
How to Start a Business Now!

LOTWINA FARODOYE

Fruitful Business: How to Start a Business Now!
Written by Lotwina Farodoye
Edited by Liz Broomfield
Cover Image by Kudrayashka

Disclaimer
This book is not intended to provide personal financial, legal, or investment advice. The Author and Publisher disclaim any liability, loss or risk, which is incurred as a consequence directly or indirectly of the use and application of any contents of this book.

This book is unique because it contains true life events and real examples from the Author's personal and business experience. In order to maintain confidentiality and respect those involved, the author has in some parts endeavoured to omit or change names, places and other minor details while maintaining the integrity of this book.

CONTENTS

ACKNOWLEDGEMENTS

I'd like to thank so many people, but first and foremost, I thank you for taking the time to pick up this book and read it. It's my pleasure to share the secrets behind my award-winning business with you in this 'How to Guide.'

Thank you to my wonderful parents, Beulah and David Samufonda. Without you none of this would have been possible. The love and encouragement that you've shown me throughout my life has been tremendous. I can't say enough about you.

Thank you team Farodoye: David, Benjamin and Jemima. Living life with you is joyful. I dedicate this book to you.

Thank you beta readers; Prudence Shapcott, Ashling Cullen, Charley Newnham, Bukki Ajayi and Indra Okonji, David Bowen for your helpful feedback on this book.

Finally, thank you Evis Akinsanya, David Cross, Joseph Farodoye, Gwen Berry, Helen Stark, Mindy Gibbins Klein, Friends, Family, Cedar Cell, Springfield and everyone who has provided support up front or behind the scenes.

ABOUT THE AUTHOR

Lotwina Farodoye is an award-winning businesswoman, sought-after public speaker and business consultant. A regular contributor to television and radio, Lotwina encourages people to unleash their potential and pursue their business dreams.

After working in the corporate business world for several years Lotwina was made redundant at the height of the recession in 2008. This knockback was the impetus for her to start her own business.

Lotwina's new enterprise rapidly took off, and her brand of natural fruit bars achieved nationwide distribution within the major supermarkets and thousands of independent shops across Britain as well as globally online, enabling Lotwina to sell her business after just 3 years.

Since then, Lotwina has continually been asked how she managed to achieve this in such a short period of time. This prompted her to write this bare-all book. Lotwina shares with you her secrets learned from her 20 years in corporate business combined with her experience of becoming an entrepreneur and starting a successful business.

ABOUT THIS BOOK

This book details the valuable lessons I've learned through starting up my business. In particular, *Fruitful Business* is designed to show how you can start a business even if your funds are limited, because there are low cost ways to get on and get ahead without breaking the bank.

I know, because that's exactly what I achieved when I started in 2009. You'll see from reading my story that I didn't have an enormous bank loan and I do not come from a rich family. For me, succeeding in business was a result of a combination of factors. This book shares these factors.

Fruitful Business is different from the conventional 'How to' guides because in addition to 'How to', I also share 'How I did', using unique insights from my personal story and experience to prove it can be done, not just by me, but by you too.

CHAPTER 1

DROP THE 't' BECAUSE YOU CAN

....

"TURN YOUR CAN'TS INTO CANS
AND YOUR DREAMS INTO PLANS"

'Can't' is one of those words that will hold you back from achieving your entrepreneurial dreams if you allow it to. Let me elaborate. When it comes to starting a business, the most common 'can'ts' I've come across include the following:

→ *"I can't start a business because it's a recession"*

→ *"I can't start a business because my cash is limited"*

→ *"I can't start a business because I'm too old, I've left it too late..."*

→ *"I can't start a business because I have no business experience"*

→ *"I can't start a business because I have no time"*

→ *"I can't start a business because I don't know where to start"*

I could keep adding to this list, but you get the picture. The list of 'I can'ts' can be endless if you allow it to be. I know this because before I started my own business, my list of 'can'ts' was very long indeed. It included all of the above and more.

I was starting in a recession, had limited cash, felt like I had missed the boat, and had never set up a business before.

The secret to turning my 'can'ts' into cans was to turn them on their head. This way they became motivating words for action. So here is the first lesson I learned: Tackle the dream-breaking list of 'can'ts' head on and start to view the negatives as positives. This is what happened:

→ *"I can't start a business because it's a recession"* **became** *"If I can make it work during a recession, I can definitely succeed during better economic times". Indeed, the recession became the catalyst for starting my business, given the scarcity of jobs.*

→ *"I can't find a job"* **became** *"I can create my own job".*

→ *"I can't start a business because my cash is limited"* **became** *"I can start my business, and because my cash is limited, I will learn to work smarter. I will search high and low to find freely available business resources, advice and services to help fuel my business growth. I will learn money saving techniques, and where they don't exist I will create my own. Where I do have to pay, I will negotiate discounts. I will become adept at finding recession-busting ways of building my business".*

→ *"I can't start a business because I'm too old, I've left it too late..."* **became** *"I can start a business because I am older and invariably wiser". Surely over the years, I've gained valuable life experience which I can use.*

→ *"I can't start a business because there is so much I don't know"* **became** *"I can start a business and will learn as much as possible as quickly as possible". Everybody starts somewhere.*

→ *"I can't start a business because I have no time"* became *"I can start my business and will learn to use my time more effectively".*

→ *"I can't start a business because I don't know where to start"* became *"I can build a business and I'll use the things that I'm most passionate about as its foundation".*

Whatever your 'can'ts' are, I believe you can turn them into 'cans' and create a successful business. But in order to do that, you need to believe it too. Here's some food for thought to help you on your way.

Henry Ford was right when he said,

> **"Whether you think you can,
> or you think you can't, you're right."**
>
> **- Henry T Ford**

YOU CAN START NOW

Don't let the state of the economy stop you whether it's boom time or bust. Some of the most successful businesses in the world were started in a recession.

The recession of 1973 to 1975 saw university dropout Bill Gates start a small company in Albuquerque developing computer languages. Today, Microsoft Windows and Office products are found on the majority of computers worldwide, resulting in annual revenue into the billions.

Revlon Cosmetics was founded in 1932 during the Great Depression. Brothers, Charles and Joseph Revlon, introduced their opaque nail varnish to the world and within just six years it had become a multi-million dollar business.

Burger King with its flame grilled burgers is another recession start-up. It began in 1954, when James McLamore and David Edgerton opened a burger restaurant in Miami. Today, Burger King operates in over 65 countries across the world.

YOU CAN BE AN ENTREPRENEUR! THERE ARE NO LIMITS

Over the years, I've heard the phrase 'The sky is the limit' used time and time again. I've even been known to use this phrase myself, but as I've progressed on my career journey, I've felt the need to re-evaluate that phrase and curtail my use of it. I now believe that there are no limits except those you place on yourself.

Ordinary people achieve extraordinary feats, and necessity really is the mother of invention. Imagine the poverty stricken child abroad who with limited education, living on the streets or in a ghetto creates a living from discarded scrap metal, other people's waste, and anything else he can find.

Whatever your start point, young, old, rich, poor, experienced, inexperienced, educated, uneducated, I believe you can create a successful business, but you need to believe it too. Your success begins with your thoughts. Therefore, start to think positively about yourself, your skills and your potential. Blast away any negative thoughts, doubts and fears by telling yourself that you can.

YOU CAN START YOUR OWN BUSINESS AT ANY AGE!

It doesn't matter how old or how young you are when you start your own business. Your age is immaterial. The main thing is that you start.

> *"You are never too old to start a new goal or dream a new dream"* – CS Lewis

In my capacity as a business consultant, I met Zandra Johnson, who became a client of mine. She started her award-winning children's furniture business, Fairy Tale Furniture, at the age of 65 and is still going strong; full of life, full of ideas and not afraid of learning new technology to empower herself and her business. Starting late has not been a barrier to her. Rather than a negative, Zandra has used her age as one of her biggest strengths to gain fantastic marketing and PR coverage for her business. She has appeared on national television and in the press numerous times as an advocate for 'oldtrepreneurs.' Zandra loves being MD at Fairy Tale Furniture as it allows her to express her passion, creativity and energy, and she has no plans to quit any time soon.

YOU CAN BUILD RELATIONSHIPS AND CREATE NETWORKS

You don't need to be well connected to start a business. You can build networks and contacts as you go along. This will help your business journey go further faster, because you'll meet people whom you can bounce ideas off, exchange knowledge with and develop mutually beneficial business relationships.

There are hundreds of places to build networks. Local business groups, entrepreneurs' clubs and 'meet-ups' are a great way to start. Search for business networks in your local area and you will find them. You can conduct the search via the internet using keywords such as 'business clubs', 'entrepreneur groups', 'networking groups' 'meet-ups' etc.

While some entrepreneur groups have joining fees, many are free to attend, and will meet regularly in your local area or a commutable distance. Each club will have its own format. For example, a number will be breakfast clubs, others meet during the day and some in the evening, so you're bound to find one that suits your schedule. If you are a little apprehensive about going alone, don't let this put you off. Why not ring up or email the administrator of the business club/network to let them know the date you plan on trying them out. This way they can look out for you and introduce you to their members when you arrive. You are bound to meet people in the same boat as you who are new too, so take courage. It really is worth getting out of your comfort zone, and the more you do it, the easier it becomes. Once you join these clubs, you'll be able to interact with the people you meet and learn useful tips along the way.

You can also network from the comfort of your own home using business-orientated internet sites such as *LinkedIn*. Here you can connect with like-minded people in your field via a range of online discussion forums and communities which are useful for asking questions and receiving advice. In addition to *LinkedIn*, there are a number of other business based websites, with new ones are springing up all the time, so you can exercise choice as to which sites will be most beneficial to you.

YOU CAN START YOUR BUSINESS ANYWHERE!
CUSTOMERS, STAFF AND RESOURCES ARE
JUST A FEW CLICKS AWAY

You can start your business operating from your own home and still reach thousands of people worldwide. We live in a global village. The internet has brought us closer together. This means that you can have customers around the globe ordering your products online 24 hours a day.

It's not just the big companies that have the luxury of outsourcing large chunks of their operations overseas in order to reduce their costs. As an individual, you also have the ability to hire 'virtual' staff over the internet to perform various functions for your business, paid for by the hour at extremely competitive rates. A whole host of websites have recently emerged which specialise in providing 'pay per hour' employees who undertake all types of work, ranging from ad hoc projects, reviewing business plans to administration, accounting, secretarial and promotional services. Using staff as and when you need them will give you flexibility while also negating the need for you to maintain premises and the expense of hiring full-time staff. On my website **www.fruitful-business.com** I've included a list of websites where you can find professionals who will undertake projects for as little as a fiver. I am constantly updating this list on my website as new resources emerge so please feel free to check it out.

YOU CAN CREATE THE TIME BY MAKING
YOUR SCHEDULE WORK FOR YOU

> *"You will never find time for anything. If you want time you must make it."* – Charles Buxton

We've all heard the phrase 'time flies'. The good news is that you are the pilot and in charge of how you spend your time.

You are already a multi-tasker. The daily activities you undertake, whether that involves going out to work or managing the home or both, automatically mean that you are used to juggling time. Waking up, preparing for the day, undertaking your daily activities, relaxing are all based on the 24 hour clock. Successful entrepreneurs eat like you, work like you, look after their families like you, and relax just like you. Yet they manage to build a successful business in addition to all of these things that they have to do daily.

The key to succeeding in the time stakes is to plan ahead and be disciplined. Schedule a time in the day that you are going to devote to creating your successful business. For example this could be during your lunch break. Imagine how far you would get if you added these hours up over a year and committed them to progressing your business venture. During your lunch break you could commit to researching your market (reading what's out there in your chosen product category, making connections in that category, etc.) Build in more time. For example the time you spend watching television or reading novels, and suddenly the time available to you to pursue your business goals increases.

Every person worldwide is governed by the 24 hour clock, including the most successful entrepreneurs. A sprinter recognises that the difference between a world record breaking performance and mediocrity lies in seconds. Make every second count.

YOU ALREADY HAVE WHAT IT TAKES TO GET STARTED

People who become successful entrepreneurs are just like you. You have skills, knowledge and experience that you've gained in your life to date that you can turn into a thriving business. You have the capacity to think wonderful thoughts, come up with ideas, connect with people, and make good decisions.

All of the purchasing choices you've made so far in life make you the ideal candidate for becoming an entrepreneur. The food you eat, the clothes you wear, the books you read, your hobbies, employment and/or home life. You've already acquired a great deal of knowledge, because you take time and effort in making them.

The products and services you buy including books, CDs, clothes, shoes, food, treatments, therapies, entertainment, lifestyle accessories etc., are all things that are making other people money right now. The same things could become income streams for you. You are already an expert because you take time and effort to research and make your choices.

When you choose a book to read, you browse the book store, library or internet and make your selection based on a number of things: whichever genre you like; what's new out there; what people are talking about or recommending as the next great read; how the book cover looks; what the summary says it will deliver and so forth.

Now, here's the key question. Do you ever think that with some of the books you've read, you could have written them yourself? Those cupcakes that you bought, could you have made them taste better, smell better, look better? Chances are that if you think so, you probably could have done. So what's stopping you from converting the things you are knowledgeable about into cash?

The only difference between you and the person that does is action. So why not start now and make a plan!

Exercise 1 is aimed at helping you to turn your 'can'ts' into 'cans' and your dreams into plans. It will help you to put behind all that's stopping or has stopped you so far.

EXERCISE 1: DROP THE 't' BECAUSE YOU CAN

1. *Make a list of things that have stopped you starting, or progressing, your business up to now*

2. *Look at each item on the list and review it in a positive light*

3. *Re-write the list, but this time turn each item into a positive statement*

---

4. *Read your new positive list aloud - boldly*

5. *Review your current time use. Identify slots of time that you are going to use to progress your business ideas*

6. *Make a verbal and written commitment to sticking to those slots you've allocated*

MY STORY

Starting your own business wasn't something that happened in my world, before I went ahead and did it. I was born in a Zimbabwean shanty town and arrived in Britain aged 3, unable to speak English. My parents had responded to a request for nurses to relocate to the UK and work for the National Health Service. My parents were hardworking people and wanted a better life for us, so they embarked on the challenge and moved our family, including my three older sisters and I, to England.

So I went from a shanty town in Zimbabwe, to a rundown sink estate in South London. I can still smell the unsavoury stench lingering in the stairwells. This was the early 1970s and there were very few black families on the estate. I remember being spat on, punched and kicked by young boys who did this for their amusement and waking up to the scrawl of bright red graffiti angrily daubed all over our front door: "NF", "Niggers go home", "Wogs Out No Doubt". Time and time again, my Dad would paint over it, only for it to reappear as soon as the paint had dried.

Where I lived, almost everyone smoked from around the age of 11 onwards, and many sniffed glue in the square. Quite a few of the girls I grew up with became teenage mums. I attended the most notorious school in the borough. I always wanted to go to one of the 'nicer' schools, so I studied hard, the ethic in our home being 'you only get what you work for'. I still studied really hard and pressed my parents to apply but I never did get accepted. I struggled to understand why I'd been rejected. Looking back, I now understand that where we lived was way beyond the catchment area for the 'nice' schools.

My parents were pretty strict and instilled the value of education in us. "Education, Education" was all they ever talked about. So much so, that as we grew up, my siblings and I knew that whatever else we would achieve in the UK we had to aim for a university degree. So I studied hard through my 'O' levels, retaking some along the way, through to 'A' levels, which I scraped through, and finally to University. This achievement heralded a real awakening of my talents. Because I chose a topic that I was passionate about and continued to work hard, I achieved a first class Honours degree. This was the start of my career in food marketing, where I worked for both huge business corporations and small companies. Wherever I worked, I applied myself as much as I could, learned as much as I could and always sought to progress towards that next level promotion. I enjoyed my work immensely.

Then I was made redundant just as the recession deepened further. It felt like the rug had been unceremoniously yanked from beneath my feet. Being made redundant in the middle of a recession and just before Christmas made finding another job in my field difficult as people were being laid off in droves. I was at my lowest ebb, dealing with a range of emotions which encompassed; anger, rejection and despair to varying degrees. My turning point came when I arrested those negative thoughts and refused to ponder them any longer. Rather than continue to dwell on the negative, I asked myself positive questions, such as:

→ *"What am I passionate about?"*

→ *"What skills have I acquired to date that I can utilise?"*

→ *"Who can help me?"*

→ *"How can I make my resources stretch?"*

→ *"What are my next steps?"*

Taking on this more positive perspective enabled me to redirect my energies from the anxiety and self-pity I'd initially felt when made redundant, to pondering a myriad of possibilities. Instead of something awful, I began to see the redundancy as a blessing and one of life's rare opportunities to take stock, and fashion a new path.

I came to the stark realisation that either I could allow the phrase, "I can't" to surreptitiously hinder my life and hamper my progress or, alternatively, I could challenge it. The choice was mine. I chose the latter. The 't' in 'can't' needed to be booted right out of my life, and I 'was wearing the boots'. I was determined to make the new situation work for me rather than against me. I searched deep within and scrutinised my thinking. I realised that the 'can'ts' that were stopping me were the very same 'cans' that would help me.

I can honestly say that creating the right mind set by turning my thoughts away from defeat to optimism, gave me the courage I needed to embark on my new business journey. I allowed myself to believe that if I couldn't get a new job, I would create my own.

CHAPTER 2

HOW TO CHOOSE YOUR PRODUCT OR SERVICE

"YOUR PASSION IS KEY"

YOUR PASSION IS KEY

A successful business can be built from practically any product or service. Walking down the high street, perusing the store aisles or surfing the internet just go to show the enormous array of products and services that people are successfully building businesses from.

The secret to choosing the right product or service for you to create your business from lies in your passion. That's key. When starting a business, choosing a product or service that you are passionate about will increase your chance of success. Instead of a chore, creating your business becomes an activity that you enjoy, create the time for and look forward to. When times get tough, your passion will help to see you through. When communicating about your business with potential customers, clients and business partners your passion will shine through and ignite their interest.

HOW TO DISCOVER YOUR PASSION

You might be at home and wondering whether there is more to life and whether you could be an entrepreneur. You may be in a job right now, asking yourself whether you could start out alone. You may be self-employed, at home, or simply wanting more. Whatever your current situation, you can make money from the things you enjoy doing. There's something satisfying in making a living from what you love doing, so finding your passion is key.

Finding your true passion may seem a little tricky, especially if you enjoy a wide range of pursuits or happen to be interested in a number of different activities. It is, however, essential that you discover it, because pursuing avenues that you are not zealous about could leave you exhausted and frustrated and may mean you fizzle out when the going gets tough.

A great exercise to help you find your ideal product or service would be to start by asking yourself what things you are really passionate about and make a list. Give each item stars according to just how enthusiastic you are about it. For example, your list could look like this:

→ *Golf* ***
→ *Pets* *
→ *Food* **
→ *Sailing* **
→ *Children* *

Three stars next to golf indicates how passionate you are about golf whereas one star means you are only moderately passionate about pets.

HOW TO DRILL DOWN FURTHER

Scrutinise your list and ask yourself what it is exactly that makes you passionate about each item. For example, if it's golf that you are really passionate about, why? Is it about being outdoors? Is it the competitive nature of the game? The skill involved? The challenge? Or that you've acquired more knowledge about golf than your friends and family?

Answering the why questions will help you to determine which direction will take. For example; a passion for playing golf could lead you to become a golf coach. However, if the reason you love golf is its outdoor nature rather than the game itself, you may be able to look to other outdoor activities to create your business and not necessarily be restricted to golf. If it's the skill and knowledge of the game that you love, you could capitalise on this in so many ways, for example: set up a website; create an online golf community that shares golf knowledge on kit, players, merchandise, skills, upcoming events etc. Using your love for the skill and knowledge of this game in this way then opens up further opportunities for affiliate marketing.

> *What's affiliate marketing?* This is where companies that produce golf courses or golf merchandise might pay you to advertise on the golf related website or online community that you have created. Every click by your followers from your website to their website gives you money because advertising money always goes where the eyeballs go. If your followers buy anything that you as an affiliate are advertising, you get commission. The more people you have subscribing to your website, the more advertising and commission based revenue you can generate.

Your passion for the skill and knowledge of the game could also lead you to create products from your knowledge such as training materials, books, CDs, DVDs and 'webinars'. Therefore one passion such as golf can lead to several different business opportunities such as coaching, training, creating products, sharing knowledge. The course of action and further development of your golf business depends on your skills, talents and strengths.

You can apply this thinking to any business or service. For example, if your passion is baking, drill down to why you are passionate about it and marry that with your skills. For example if your strengths are explaining or teaching, could you run courses or workshops to teach others? Could you teach others on line? If you love baking and you have literary strengths or skills could you produce a cookbook? If you love baking and want to sell products could you find outlets for your merchandise and look for a partner manufacturer to help you upscale your production? The possibilities are endless. So really drill down and keep asking yourself the 'Why' questions so that whatever type of business you choose to pursue, you are clear about your passion as well as your skills, talents and strengths as these will determine the best direction for your business to take. When you marry your passion with your strengths, talents and skills you have a winning combination.

How do I identify to your skills, strengths and talents?
Make a list of your skills, strengths and talents. Then review these in relation to how you could use those skills, strengths and talents to take your passion forward. Don't be afraid to ask friends, family and colleagues to help you. Those closest to you can often recognize abilities in you that you have overlooked or take for granted. They might just help put the spotlight on skills that you could utilise that you are underutilizing or haven't even considered.

Exercise 2 will help you to clarify what your passion, skills and strengths are.

EXERCISE 2: **WHAT'S MY PASSION AND WHAT ARE MY STRENGTHS, SKILLS AND TALENTS?**

1. *Make a list of the things you are passionate about. By passionate I mean the things you really enjoy, get excited about, or love to talk about. These are the things that you actively seek out information on and*

like to be updated about. If you had a free day off, chances are you would allocate time to it. Include in the list hobbies, business, personal and general interest.

2. *Put stars next to each item on your list, to indicate how passionate you are: one star equals passionate, three stars equals extremely passionate.*

3. *Revisit the item(s) with the most stars. List the reasons why you are passionate about them.*

4. *Think about the methods you could employ to generate an income from your passions and list them. For example could you source and sell products related to your passion? Could you create your own products for sale related to your passion, such as books, DVDs, etc.? Could you teach, coach or train others about these areas?*

5. *Play to your strengths. Make a list of the skills, talents and strengths that you have. Don't be afraid to ask friends and family to help you draw up your list. Those closest to you are often in a position to help you discover where your talents lie and might just help put the spotlight on skills that you could use that you hadn't even considered.*

6. *Review your skills, strengths and talents in the light of your passion. Think through how you can marry these to your passion?*

7. *Write down a sentence or two outlining how you propose to take your passion forward using the skills, talents and strengths from the list you've drawn up.*

HOW TO GET A HEAD START: DON'T REINVENT THE WHEEL IF YOU DON'T NEED TO

People often assume that to start a successful business you need a totally new idea or concept. Although it is a great thing to be able to do that, most businesses are created out of existing ideas or services but simply implemented better, or targeted to a new market, updated, improved, marketed better and so forth.

"GIVE IT SOME CREATIVE WELLY"

For example, wellington boots are not a new invention. Wellies have been around for years, historically worn by rural communities, farmers and labourers and available in dark colours such as black, navy blue or green. Recently formed, forward-thinking companies have taken this dated concept and updated it creating modern funky looking wellington boots in fashionable bright colours. These new colours and styles are appealing to younger people, the fashion conscious, and the festival crowds. By improving an existing product, these up-and-coming companies have appealed to a new target market, giving wellies a wider appeal and helping the product to experience a renaissance.

In terms of the business you decide to set up, I can tell that you everything that's currently being done out there can be done better by you, through researching your market, understanding the gaps, and making significant improvements to meet customer needs. There are so many great businesses out there, but they're not fulfilling their potential because they are not optimising their offer, their marketing is not reaching the market or they are tired.

HOW TO START FAST: FIND THE GAPS

Have you ever been in that situation when you've wanted to buy or use something but you just can't find it in the shops or online? In other words, there is a 'gap' in the market and in some instances a gaping hole! These gaps in the market often represent great business opportunities and are just waiting to be filled with products and services from savvy entrepreneurs such as you. Can you fill the gaps in your marketplace with your product or business idea?

HOW TO START WELL: SOLUTION-ORIENTATED THINKING

Have you ever been frustrated with an existing product or service that you've used and wished it had better features or operated differently? Have you ever been disappointed by the choice available, service delivery, content or other aspects of a product or service you currently use? If so, your negative experience could be the catalyst you need to come up with your own solutions and make a successful business out of them. Furthermore, other people are likely to have experienced the same frustrations, those same people become ready customers for your solution oriented product or service.

CONSIDER SCALABILITY

When you choose your business model, think about its potential for growth and income generation. For example, if you plan to provide a service such as life coaching, more often than not you are required to be physically present to coach your clients, whether that be face to face, over the phone or by some other method of communication. The number of clients you can take on is limited to how many you can see or speak to in one day. If, however, you can develop products from your advice, such as books, webinars or DVDs, your income generation model becomes scalable and your ability to reach a wider audience is no longer confined to the limits of your physical presence. Your products can be purchased from a wide range of sources without you being there. Your income generation has the potential to soar.

More interestingly, with a scalable business model, you can literally 'make money while you sleep'.

> *How can I make money while I sleep?* Once you have put in all the effort required to produce your product, you do not physically have to be present while customers are purchasing it. Indeed you might be asleep, on holiday, or doing more of the things you love. This is because people can buy your products via the shops or over the internet without you being physically present.

The same is true of any physical product you make. For example, selling jams at a market stall, fair or car boot sale requires you to be present. However, a more scalable way of selling those jams would be do so via wholesalers, shops, supermarkets and online giving you access to more customers and drastically scaling up your earnings.

Scalability can be built into every business model, so think through how you might build this into your business plan.

TOP TIPS: HOW TO CHOOSE YOUR BUSINESS

1. *Choose something you are really passionate about. Your passion will sustain you through the ups and downs.*

2. *Draw up a list of your skills and talents. Friends and family can help.*

3. *There's no need to reinvent the wheel unless you want to. You can always do things differently by putting your own unique spin on it, or simply better by understanding your target audience and tailoring your proposition to meet their needs.*

---

4. *Find the gaps in your marketplace. They could represent a significant business opportunity for you.*

5. *Turn your frustrations into solutions. Doing things better can also represent a great business opportunity.*

6. *Choose a business option that is scalable and does not depend on you being physically present. This will result in your reach becoming wider.*

MY STORY

HOW I FOUND MY PASSION

When I started my award-winning business, I began with my life long interest in food. As a child, I relished helping mum in the kitchen. I enjoyed going to the supermarkets to choose our food and always had a fascination with the amazing dishes Mum would make out of very simple ingredients. I chose to study Food Management and Marketing because that seemed the natural choice for me. Because I was engrossed in the topic, I excelled in it. Once I started a regular job, I made a beeline for food companies, working first in meat, then pizza, then bread, then nuts and dried fruit and loved each of these jobs equally.

After years of being quite successful, I was made redundant as the company I was working for became a casualty of the harsh economic climate. Suddenly I had no job. The recession was biting and the jobs for which I'd trained became scarce. I felt worried, sick, and angry that I could be so easily dispensed with, given the hard work, knowledge and effort that I'd put into the job. I'd given 100% but that didn't seem to matter. I felt awful, ashamed, and downtrodden. I was even embarrassed to tell people that I'd lost my job and for a while I couldn't sleep at night wondering what I would do next. How would I earn a living for my family?

On one such sleepless night, as I pondered these questions, I asked myself what I was passionate about. The light bulb moment came. Bingo! Food. I was passionate about food. That had not changed since my childhood, and all through the years that I'd worked with food, no matter for which company or in what post. I also asked myself questions such as what I'd learned along the way, and what skills did I have that I could use to go forward.

From that point on, I began to believe that I could go forward regardless of whether any company would employ me. In the absence of a job, I decided to create my own and got really excited about the idea of starting my own company. Once I started listing my passions and skills, my thoughts came thick and fast. I started to become confident and really believe in myself. It was obvious that I'd always loved food. I believed that I could start a business on the basis of my passion and skills. Of course I still needed to acquire a number of other skills, as I'd never worked for myself before, but that was not going to stop me.

HOW I GOT A HEAD START BY FINDING THE GAPS AND USING SOLUTION ORIENTATED THINKING

When I started my business, I chose the concept of natural fruit bars. I was attracted to the idea of natural fruit bars because of the difficulties I've had in finding healthy snacks in the shops to give my children that they will actually eat. Whenever I go shopping with the family, my children ask for chocolate bars, sweets and crisps and I feel like a tyrant when I say they can't have them. I often thought that it would be great to have healthier alternatives that looked and tasted yummy alongside the chocolate bars, to give people more choice. The more I spoke to other mums about this, the more I realised I was not alone. After speaking to several of mums in the playground, in my street, at church, at the shops, the idea for my range of natural fruit bars was born.

HOW I GOT A FAST START BY NOT REINVENTING THE WHEEL

I certainly didn't reinvent the wheel. I took a well-established recipe from Scandinavia and brought it to a new market in the UK where there was a huge gap and significant business opportunity. I introduced the bar to a whole new audience who'd never tried it before. My product was already the top-selling fruit bar in Scandinavia. Having identified a gap in the UK market, and conducted my research, I knew that the Scandinavian fruit bar had the potential to be a success in the UK for a number of reasons.

Firstly, timing: in the UK, the trends were moving towards a healthier style of living and eating. Statistics showed obesity becoming an increasing threat to the nation's health with nearly a quarter of adults predicted to be in the obese category in the next decade. In my own way, I wanted to help address this. by bringing to the market a healthy snacking range. Secondly, I felt that my product range had a significant unique selling point versus existing snacks on the market because my products were 100% natural, i.e. no added salt, no added sugar, no artificial additives, while the other 'healthy' snack products were full of additives.

HOW I MADE SCALABILITY MY GOAL FROM THE ONSET

One of my main business goals was to get my products into the major supermarkets and available on the internet, which I succeeded in doing. Rather than confine myself to selling my fruit bars from a market stall, trade fair or locations where I'd have to be physically present, I targeted the supermarkets, because I knew that as a nation, we buy over 90% of our food from them. Getting my product into the supermarkets was key to ensuring that my sales growth was scalable far beyond what I could achieve alone. I sought out the supermarkets because many of them are open 24 hours a day. People could literally buy my products at the supermarkets but I didn't need to be there to hand the products over to them. The supermarkets have shops in places all over the country, which would extend my sales significantly, as I didn't need to be physically there when a shopper placed my products into their shopping basket. It was the same rationale for the internet. I achieved listings for my products on various websites including one of the largest distributors in the world. This meant that sales of my products were no longer confined to the limits of my physical presence, but people the world over could buy my products at the click of a button. I was making money while I slept!

CHAPTER 3

HOW TO BRIDGE THE GAP

"ENHANCE YOUR KNOWLEDGE AND THRIVE"

So, you've chosen what you're passionate about, reviewed your skill, strength and talents, and you've got lots of enthusiasm. You might even have some experience in your specialist field whether that's head knowledge, practical experience or both. However, there might still be a knowledge gap where you lack skills or confidence in other areas. For example, you might be brilliant at baking cakes but you lack the knowledge of how to get these cakes to market. You might be passionate about fly fishing or coaching people but you lack the knowledge of how to attract customers who will buy your expertise. You might be passionate about childcare but don't know the laws surrounding starting a childcare business. This chapter gives you top tips on how to acquire knowledge and expertise in record time and at little or zero cost.

HOW TO TAP INTO OTHER PEOPLE'S KNOWLEDGE

> *"None of us is as smart as all of us."*
> **- Ken Blanchard**

Think of all of the people you know or have ever come across. This could be at any time in your life, and any place. You may be surprised first at the sheer number of people you know, but also at their wide range of expertise. In addition to the people we've come face to face with, there are others who we know, or have knowledge of through our friends, family, neighbours, colleagues, hobbies, general interest groups, or acquaintances.

If you're a member of any social networks, for example *LinkedIn* groups, you could you ask on there if anyone can help you out? People will often help you out for free, especially if you're a relative, or a friend and they know you are just starting your venture.

HOW TO LOOK FOR 'WIN WIN' SITUATIONS

People's motivation to help you without receiving financial recompense can often stem from a personal connection, but also in many instances a 'win win' scenario. For example, they may anticipate that if they help you while you are a start-up, as your business takes off and you grow, you are more likely to be happy to pay for their services, since they helped you out initially. Also, you might publicise their good work by recommending them to others and bringing them paying clients in this manner.

Another 'win win' reason that they might help could be that they are starting out themselves and want clients to give them good references for their own services. For example, a recent graduate in web design might be looking for case studies to practice their skills. Building your website gives them an opportunity to implement their training and showcase their work (your newly built website) to prospective clients and subsequently get paid by their new clients.

Garnering help and support from people is often easier when you identify and discuss a 'win win' scenario that is beneficial for both parties.

EXERCISE 3: HOW TO TAP INTO OTHER PEOPLE'S KNOWLEDGE

1. *Think about your circle of friends, their friends, close family and distant family members. Each person you list has skills that they have acquired in their own life journeys, studies, jobs or hobbies.*

2. *Make a list of these friends and family members. Don't just include immediate friends; list their friends too and their children.*

3. *Next to the names of friends and family write down what you know of them in relation to their skills and/or areas of expertise. For example, one of your relatives or friends might be pretty good with computers or have studied computers at college. Alternatively, they might have a son/daughter who is good with computers.*

4. *Evaluate your list of people and their skills and determine whether any of them could help you out. This could involve giving you advice in their area of expertise when you need it or acting as a sounding board. The help they give might even go further than that, depending on what it is you ask for.*

5. *Don't be afraid to ask for help. People are more often than not willing to assist. The level of assistance will vary. Some may step in themselves and be hands on, while others will point you in the direction of those who can help or guide you to where you can obtain further resource.*

6. *Try to create a 'win-win' scenario. For example, in exchange for their help, could you publicise their company or skills on your website?*

HOW TO NETWORK

Networking is about building mutually beneficial business relationships. It's about getting to know people with a view to exchanging knowledge or assistance. Networking will help you to get further faster.

What is networking? Networking in its simplest form is connecting with other people for the purpose of growing your business. There are so many ways to do this and so many groups you can visit or join in order to make connections. There are a large number of groups where you can network, for example women's groups, men's groups, general business groups, entrepreneurs' groups, meet ups. On my website **www.fruitful-business.com** I list a range of groups by name and location and continuously update that list so please feel free to draw from it.

In addition to regular networking groups and forums, there are also many ad hoc business events, trade shows and interest groups in your specialist field which are all free to sign up to, where you can meet like-minded people as well as people with different skill sets.

NETWORKING WORKS BEST WHEN

→ *You go to events with an open mind, ready to talk to people from all walks of life.*

→ *You're willing to share about yourself, your background or your journey and listen to others, too.*

→ *You're prepared to help people and ask what it is you can do for them: you may have the type of connection in your circle that they need to access and vice versa.*

➡ *You exchange contact details in order to continue any relevant conversations further down the line*

As you keep in touch with the people you meet, you widen your chance of success. Through networking, you might gain an introduction to a business that you are trying to approach or a name of someone you can write to or email.

It's okay to feel nervous about attending events in order to strike up conversations with complete strangers. It can feel a bit awkward and may take some getting used to. The potential rewards however are worth it. It's okay to feel nervous. If you are, practice introducing yourself and your business at home in front of the mirror or, with a friend beforehand. Practice making your introduction of yourself and business interesting, and to the point. This is often referred to as the 'elevator pitch'.

HOW TO PREPARE YOUR 'ELEVATOR PITCH'

A good elevator pitch should last no more than 20 to 30 seconds, the typical length of a ride in an elevator or lift.

How do I start the conversation? Often a simple introductory sentence from you such as "Do you mind if I join you?" works really well at opening up a discussion to include yourself. Or simply introducing yourself to people works really well: "Hi, my name is Jo Bloggs, what's yours?" Soon you'll be chatting about your areas of expertise and how you can mutually benefit one another. They may have spoken to somebody earlier in the evening who can help you even if they themselves cannot and vice versa.

Why do I need business cards? Have you ever been in that situation when somebody asks you for your contact details and you are frantically digging around in your handbag or pockets for a scrap of paper to write them on? Depending on the contents of your handbag or pockets, that can be a little embarrassing at best and looks unprofessional at worst. To avoid this it often helps to carry business cards with you to any networking event you attend because they enable you to provide your details neatly and quickly.

Even if you are only in the ideas phase of your start-up and don't have a company name or logo, you can still have business cards made with simply your name, email address, contact number and field of business or area of expertise. Getting business cards made up in this way is relatively simple and needn't cost the earth. An internet search will highlight many companies that even provide business cards for free and you just pay postage and packaging. I have included some of these on my website **www.fruitful-business.com**

HOW TO KEEP IN TOUCH

When you get given a business card, always make a point of following it up after your initial meeting with an email to say how much you enjoyed meeting that person. You may not need them now, but a time may come further down the line where you may need to call them. And vice versa: if they need to call you, they'll feel more confident doing so if you've continued to extend the hand of friendship after your initial meeting. Once you have their business card or details you can look them up on business networking sites such as *LinkedIn* and send them a request to connect based on your meeting at the networking event. They're likely to remember you, especially if you've followed up with a friendly email. Once you're accepted onto their *LinkedIn*, that opens up an even wider range of people to you. People are doing this the world over, and never before have so many contacts been so easily accessible.

Networking really can open doors to contacts that you never thought you could access: those supermarket buyers, that golfing group, that coaching school really can be accessible and just a few contacts away.

Once you start networking regularly, introducing yourself and starting conversations gets easier. You might even find it enjoyable!

TOP TIPS: NETWORKING

1. *Don't be afraid to join in the conversation or start a new one. Most people are in the same boat as you and welcome a discussion.*

2. *Make sure you take business cards with you to the networking event. This makes giving out your contact details neat and quick. Business cards are often free on the internet, where all you pay is postage.*

3. *When you are given a business card, follow it up with an email to say how much you enjoyed meeting the person and to ask if you can become a connection on further business forums such as LinkedIn.*

WORKSHOPS, SEMINARS AND SHORT COURSES

There are a staggering number of free and low cost workshops and seminars out there run by government bodies and their affiliates. They have a vested interest in running them, as they understand that small business are vital to a thriving economy. Topics are wide ranging but can be applied to most businesses, for example taxation, VAT, marketing, intellectual property law, branding, market research, and accounting.

Organisations running these courses in the UK include The British library Business and IP Centre and the HMRC.

The beauty of these workshops, seminars and courses is that they are short, typically half a day or a day. These enable you to fill your knowledge gaps and hit the ground running without having to go back to formal studying, unless of course that's what you want to do. Many of these workshops, seminars and short courses are free, because they are funded by the government and their affiliates in order to help ordinary people start-up businesses and kick start the economy. By signing up for these courses, you can get access to real expert knowledge without having to pay the hefty fees yourself.

As well as government-funded courses, private companies often run free short courses and seminars. These courses and taster sessions might be more specific to an industry, product or service, for example photography, baking, etc. They do this because you might end up paying for a longer course or purchase their course materials. Often these free taster courses are packed with great basic starter knowledge which can often be useful in itself and provide you with clarity on a certain matter before you shell out for a full-blown course.

Wherever you are in the world, if you search the internet for free courses and workshops, you'll come up with a range of them: they are definitely out there so do your research and ask around.

TOP TIPS: ENHANCING YOUR KNOWLEDGE

1. *Invest in your knowledge and skills by attending the training you need. It's well worth it.*

---

2. *There is so much free training available. I have included a list of free business training workshops on my website* **www.fruitful-business.com**

3. *A great deal of training is short. So try out a few and see what you can learn – and what contacts you can make.*

MY STORY

When I started my business I had passion and a strong set of skills in my chosen area of expertise but lacked a whole range of knowledge and skills in other areas. Although I clearly knew about food, sales and marketing, having spent 20 years working my way up to senior levels within this field, I lacked legal knowledge, accounting skills, production expertise and so forth. This is because I had always been an employee and my job role was narrowly defined to my areas of competence. Food and marketing was my comfort zone. I was not required to undertake other functions such as company law, accounts, administration, secretarial, production and so forth, because the big companies I worked for employed their own lawyers, accountants, secretaries, production, quality control staff and a whole host of other functions.

As a result, when starting my own business, I felt I had a huge lack of skills and knowledge. The prospect of starting my own business without any of this knowledge was daunting. I also had very little time and money to acquire the extra skills I needed. However, the fact that I'd got both my mind and heart set on starting a business went a long way in helping me overcome my knowledge gaps. Thinking about turning my 'can'ts' to 'cans', I became determined to acquire the knowledge I needed in record time and without a budget. To acquire the knowledge I needed, I used a combination of tactics which included:

→ *Tapping into other people's knowledge*
→ *Attending seminars short courses and workshops*
→ *Networking to engage in skills swaps*

HOW I TAPPED INTO OTHER PEOPLE'S KNOWLEDGE AND THEIR SKILL SETS

I tapped into other people's knowledge on many occasions in order to build my business. This was not only essential because of my budget constraints, but also a way of tapping into expert knowledge without ever having to become an expert myself. This is how I did it.

Early on in my business I needed a website to both increase the visibility of my products and enhance the credibility of my company. One of my dearest friends had recently trained as a web developer. Without hesitation, I approached my friend and asked her to help me out. She did so gladly. I believe this was for two reasons. The first was because we were good friends and had a long lasting personal connection. Secondly, as a newly trained web developer, my friend wanted to put into practice her newly acquired skills and needed a variety of websites to showcase her excellent work to potential new customers. A 'win-win' scenario. If I didn't have my friend, I would have approached my local college and asked the web tutors whether any of their students wanted live local business cases to work on as most web development students need to submit work they've done to pass aspects of their courses.

To help with technical knowledge and UK labelling requirements for my fruit bars, I received help from the technical director of a company I used to work for. She kindly checked my labelling to ensure that it was legal. It would have taken me considerably longer to get to grips with the legislation had I tried to understand it myself let alone applying it in the real world. Tapping into an ex-colleagues knowledge and skill set was invaluable in my situation and I was grateful for the help.

HOW I ATTENDED WORKSHOPS, SEMINARS AND SHORT COURSES

I attended numerous of seminars, workshops and short courses in a range of subjects where I needed to brush up my skills, extend my knowledge and or get up to speed really quickly. 90% of these were free. They included topics such as taxation, VAT run by the HMRC (UK Government), how to trademark your brand, how to research your market, e-commerce - buying and selling on the computer, and so on. All of these seminars gave me essential knowledge and helped me to network with people in a similar position to myself.

As well as the knowledge I gained to help drive my business forward, the seminars boosted my confidence so that I could speak the language required in my business.

CHAPTER 4

HOW TO DO YOUR OWN MARKET RESEARCH

"KNOWLEDGE IS ESSENTIAL"

KNOWLEDGE IS ESSENTIAL

Market research is essential prior to launching your product or service. In particular, good market research will help you to understand the needs of your target audience and marketplace so that you can create products and services that meet their needs and exceed their expectations.

Large organisations do market research all the time to help them to improve their existing products and services and also to help them to create new ones. They spend thousands of pounds on understanding their consumers and their marketplace because this understanding is vital to their success. That is the reason you and I are often asked to complete postal surveys, stopped in the street to answer questions or even telephoned at home. Your answers to these questions are used by successful companies to develop their strategies for growth.

HOW TO DO YOUR OWN MARKET RESEARCH

The big companies typically hire specialist research agencies to conduct their consumer and market research on their behalf. They rely on these agencies to plan and implement their research projects, which includes formulating questions, asking consumers those questions and interpreting the results. Experienced market research agencies are able to charge thousands of pounds for these services because the information they yield from their research is valuable.

If you're in the start-up phase of your business, the chances are you that you won't have thousands of pounds in market research. However, rather than not do any research at all owing to lack of funds, I've discovered through experience that there is still a lot that you can do on your own. To help me illustrate this, think back to any market research that you've ever taken part in. Have you ever been questioned in the street? Questioned over the phone? Filled in a questionnaire or survey online, in a magazine or one that's arrived in the post? Chances are the questions you answered were aimed at understanding your shopping behaviour and habits, what products and services you use, what features of those products and services are of most benefit to you, how often you buy those products or services and who else in your household uses them. I could carry on listing the types of question you may have been asked to answer, but I know you get the picture.

With this in mind, I believe that you can create your own set of information-gathering questions that will help you to understand what your target consumers want and need, and then improve your products, services and ideas accordingly. When you truly understand what your consumers are looking for, you can develop unique sales propositions (USP's) that appeal directly to them, giving you an edge over your competitors. Taking the time to ask your consumers questions will also help you to really understand your marketplace and where it's heading, so that you stay a step ahead.

HOW TO WRITE A SIMPLE QUESTIONNAIRE

Writing down questions need not be arduous. You can do this either by yourself or may find it helpful to work with a friend. Just think of everything you would like to understand about your product or service from your target consumer's perspective. For example, from the onset, you may want to know whether your target consumer would ever consider purchasing or consuming your product or service. Note it down as a question. If they would consider buying your products, why? What are the product features that appeal to them? How much would they be prepared to pay?

Finding out the reasons why they would purchase your product or service will help you see where your competitive edge lies. You could use this information in future to help you market your products, listing in the description the key benefits that consumers will gain from using them.

Alternatively, you will need answers to the opposite scenario: for example, if they wouldn't consider purchasing your product, why not? Is there anything missing from your product or service? Is anything unclear? Which other products in the marketplace do they currently purchase? Finding out this information will help you to improve your products considerably.

There are so many other questions you might want to answers. Make a note of all of them. Try and write them down in the simplest form possible. Really long, convoluted questions can be quite hard to understand, so make sure each question addresses one topic.

When you are writing down your questions, it's important not to 'lead' your consumers into giving a particular answer. This will not help your cause because you need to find out what they really think, rather than what you want them to think. A friend can help you to sense check the questions to ensure that they are easy to understand and not too leading, or indeed misleading.

Review the order of your questions to ensure a logical flow. For example, all questions about purchasing should go together. All questions about product features should go together.

Leave enough room for comprehensive answers if your questionnaires are going to be filled in by hand. If you are asking the questions yourself, leave enough space for recording the answers.

ONLINE TOOLS CAN HELP YOU TO FORMULATE YOUR QUESTIONS

There are a whole host of online survey tools that can help to put together your questionnaires for the purposes of your market research. Many of these are free at the basic level. Searching online for 'survey tools' will yield samples of free questionnaires. Looking at these free sample questions will help you to phrase your own questions correctly and adapt them to your own product or service.

You can also use online survey tools to do the complete job of putting together your questionnaires, distributing them to the email addresses you provide. Your participants can then complete your questionnaires electronically. This makes it easy for people to answer your questions when they happen to be sitting at their computer and makes the collection of results simpler and faster too – you can spread the word through social media like *Facebook*.

On my website **www.fruitful-business.com** I have a list of online survey tools which you can access. Rather than name the tools here, I like to keep the list fresh and add to it regularly so that you have the most up-to-date information at your fingertips.

TOP TIPS: DESIGNING QUESTIONNAIRES

1. *Think of all the questions you'd like to ask your target audience about your products or service.*

---

2. *Write down each question and keep it simple. Ask a friend to read through your list of questions to make sure that they are easy to understand.*

3. *Ensure that your questions are not 'leading' or designed to provide your preferred responses because it is essential to understand what your target audience really think as oppose to what you would like them to think. Open-ended questions (rather than those you can answer with yes or no) are useful for giving your participants free rein on the information they provide giving you in-depth insight.*

4. *A whole host of online survey tools are available for free from the internet. The sample questions from online survey tools can give you ideas for your own questions and also ideas of how to phrase your questions clearly, succinctly and in a non-leading way.*

5. *Online survey tools can also be used to manage the entire questionnaire process of creating, distributing and capturing responses.*

HOW TO ACCESS CONSUMERS FOR THE PURPOSE OF RESEARCH

Another of the reasons market research agencies are able to charge thousands of pounds is because they can access consumers. Typically, they are prepared to go out and find consumers and gauge their views, whether that's through stopping them on the street, cold calling their homes or setting up focus groups.

As an individual, you have access to more people than you think. You are surrounded by people - colleagues, neighbours, parents; at the school gate, Brownies, Cubs, and the various clubs you ferry your children to and from, parent and toddler groups, buddies at the golf club, pub, church members, coffee mornings, book clubs and various interest groups that you may attend. You have the potential to come into contact with dozens if not hundreds of people.

JUST ASK

Many of the people you come into contact with would be happy to take part in market research for your product or service if you asked them especially when you explain the value of their input. Generally, people enjoy giving their opinion, and will often agree to provide their views if your research is convenient to them and uncomplicated - hence the need to keep your questionnaires simple and easy to complete.

Sometimes, providing a great atmosphere may also help you to recruit people for your research. For example you can turn your research exercise into a coffee morning or a cheese and wine evening, where you provide refreshments before or after the event.

There will, of course, be people who will turn down your request to take part in your research. They may not have the time or the inclination. The main thing is not to take any refusals as personal. Just move on to asking the next person or group of people on your list until you achieve your desired number of participants.

The main thing to remember about the people you select to take part in your research is making sure that they belong to your target group for the product or service in question. For example, if your product is linked to golf performance, try asking members of the golf club you attend or people belonging to golf interest groups. People who have no interest in golf may not understand your product or service so will not be the best people to help you develop your product or service.

FOCUS GROUPS

It's a good idea to start your research on a small scale at first by conducting what is known as a focus group. In a focus group you select a handful of people to initially run your ideas by and ask your questions to.

How do I organise a focus group? I recommend a group of between 5 and 10 people. You can organise a meeting in a relaxed environment like your living room if you know the participants. However, an outside venue is just as good if you are unfamiliar with the group you have chosen. As long as your choice of venue is conducive to being able to ask questions and listen to the answers without being distracted or interrupted, it will be fine.

You'll be amazed at the richness and depth of the information you can garner from a small group of people.

RECORDING YOUR FINDINGS

It's a good idea to record the focus group if you have a camcorder or voice recorder (you even find these on smartphones these days). Always ask for permission from your participants beforehand if you are going to record them. This way you can play the footage back afterwards and be able to note down the key words or views that were communicated and refresh your mind as to what your target market's thoughts were.

Alternatively, have a friend taking notes during the session to record the group's views and responses to your key questions. This will take preparation, as you will need to type up the questions in advance, leaving a space between them, so your note taker can concentrate on and record the answers.

LARGER SCALE USING QUESTIONNAIRES

Once you have conducted initial focus groups, there may be questions that you'd like to gain a consensus on. While focus groups are useful for gaining ideas or highlighting problems they are not able to provide the whole picture because they are only comprised of a handful of people. This is where larger-scale research, known as quantitative research, may help, whereby you capture the views of the masses rather than just a few. As it's impractical to get hundreds of people involved in a discussion at the same time, the easiest way to conduct quantitative research is to develop a questionnaire that your respondents fill in. Providing a questionnaire also allows results to be compared and averages worked out.

Mining for the truth: When developing your question- naire, a ranking system for each question may also be useful, for example 1 equates to strongly agree and 5 equates to strongly disagree or an alternative system such as 1 = really dislike and 5 = really like. Run your questions by friends and family first so they can 'sense check' your questions before you try them out on your target audience.

As long as your questions do not lead or force respondents to arrive at particular conclusions, you are gathering their thoughts in the true sense of the word, i.e. their own thoughts, not imposing yours on them. This is important because you want to serve them rather than yourself. You want the whole truth. You want to unearth where the gaps are that your product or service can fill.

HONEST AND FRANK FEEDBACK IS ESSENTIAL

Be sure to explain that you are looking for frank and honest feedback. You don't want your participants to tell you only good things or what you may want to hear, nice as that may be. As a professional, you are looking for the unbiased truth. It's important to let your participants know from the start that both positive and negative comments are equally useful. Then make sure that you are prepared for both. You may be pleasantly surprised as they may come up with new ideas, uses or desires which can work to your advantage in developing your product. Alternatively, you may be unpleasantly surprised that your target audience actually dislikes aspects of your would-be product or service. If this is the case, count this a blessing, as you can make adjustments accordingly before taking the product or service to the next stage. Any positive feedback or confirmation of what you already thought you knew can be reassuring and give you the motivation that you really need in order to progress to the next stage.

MY STORY

The market research companies quoted me 20,000 to undertake my market research. I didn't have 20,000 but I knew that I needed to understand the views of my target consumers if my products were to succeed.

In the absence of funds for research, I asked my neighbours, mums I'd met at the school gate, families that attended the same church as me, friends of friends and anyone else who fitted my target audience to take part in my research. I managed to get over 200 people to provide their opinion on my products! This is how I did it:

HOW I CONDUCTED FOCUS GROUPS
AND RECORDED MY FINDINGS

I knocked on the doors of a number of my neighbours and asked them if they wouldn't mind helping me out with some research. Because my fruit bars were aimed at school lunchboxes and also mums snacking, I was quite selective in my choice of invitees, selecting mums who I knew had school age children, the key target group for my fruit bars. I felt that these mums would be most able to contribute effectively to the discussion.

I explained that a few of the other mums would also be taking part in my research and that it would be a great chance for a coffee and chat afterwards and would really help me out a great deal, as I valued their opinion. I explained the nature of my research, i.e. that I would be showing them some fruit bars and asking their opinions on taste and packaging as well as their buying habits. To my delight they were all happy to help.

Friday soon came round, the day of my first focus group. I'd made some preparations in advance by buying a few competitor products and laying them out carefully on my coffee table. I had prepared a question guide to keep the discussion on track. My questions for the focus group were quite open ended, because I didn't want to lead the group's thinking but just wanted to capture their honest thoughts.

The richness of feedback proved to be invaluable even though much of it was negative at this stage. Unfortunately, the bars that I was hoping to launch in the UK prompted a whole range of negative feedback. The answers ranged from "I don't like the packaging" to, "I would never buy those". Although I felt like they were delivering big blows and bad news, I maintained my composure. Rather than try to persuade them of the merits of my bars, I stayed professional and asked them to elaborate on why they would not purchase the bars, however painful it was to listen to. "Why wouldn't you buy them?" I probed in a calm manner. The responses came thick and fast: "The bars look cheap", "I don't like the foreign writing on them", "The packaging looks dull", "The packaging looks dated", "The image of a monkey with its finger stuck up its nose is disgusting". I felt awful listening to this feedback, but carried on without wincing.

I asked the focus group to pick up some bars from the pile that they perhaps would consider buying and also asked their reasons why. It was quite clear that appearance was key. Many picked up competitor products and talked about how they would be happy to purchase them. I asked why, and my focus group participants commented on how the competitor packaging was bright, attractive, modern and inviting.

TASTING TIME

Having gauged the group's views on the various bars, including my own, I asked the group to move to tasting the various bars and noted their comments. To make sure that my group were not overwhelmed by munching through a whole range of bars, I cut the bars into small bite size pieces and placed the pieces onto crisp white plates.

Again, lots of really insightful comments were generated from the tasting sessions For example, they absolutely loved the taste of my bars while the competitors' bars tasted artificial. This prompted some of them to enquire about the ingredients in each bar. I said they could read out exactly what the ingredients were from the pack of each bar that we'd opened to taste. They were really impressed that my bars were predominantly fruit with nothing artificial added, and shocked that competitor bars had a huge range of ingredients, many containing artificial additives with unrecognisable ingredients.

HOW I DREW CONCLUSIONS FROM MY FOCUS GROUPS

After conducting a couple more groups in the fashion described above, I noted many similarities, i.e. that the mums loved my product taste and simple ingredients but hated the packaging.

I was able to determine quite quickly from the focus group feedback that I needed to take further action on the development of my bars if they were to compete and succeed in the UK market. For example, I could not ignore the comments on packaging. I needed a complete overhaul of the product image to make the bars look more desirable for my target market.

On the upside, the focus groups helped me to realise with great clarity that my products tasted good: in fact they tasted superior to the competitor products. Another positive observation was that the groups preferred my simple ingredients to the complicated competitor bars, and that reading the labels clearly did matter. This reinforced my understanding of "natural" as one of my unique selling points (USP's) which I should communicate.

This feedback helped me to decide that I needed to get my products redesigned. it was obvious that my target audience would never purchase the bars, and experience the great taste, or even pick them up and note the natural ingredients, if they were launched in their current format.

HOW I DID LARGER SCALE RESEARCH

Now that I knew from my small focus groups that my products had a uniquely fresh taste, I wanted to know which varieties to launch. I had a choice of several varieties and flavours but decided that I needed to narrow it down to three flavours initially so as not to spread myself too thin when launching. This led me to do some larger scale research to find out which flavours my target market preferred. Together with Benjamin and Jemima, my children, who were aged 4 and 6 at the time, I formed a production line. I made up hundreds of packs of sample bars, seven flavours in each pack.

It was a very simple pack indeed. I bought neat plain white plastic bags from the pound shop and inserted the seven varieties into each one. I also included my questionnaire, which my sister had helped me design. Her help was invaluable because she phrased things in a much better way than I would have done alone. I also included in the pack a letter with the tasting instructions. In particular, participants needed to taste the bars with their whole family and record the comments and flavour ranking of each participant in the spaces provided.

The reason I included instructions on how to taste the bars and complete the questions was because I wanted to ensure uniformity and consistency in the methodology so that the results from each participant could be compared. The instructions placed in the packs also included information on when I would collected the forms and a thank you note.

HOW I ASKED

Having carefully prepared my research packs I stood outside the school gates. I was a little hesitant at first, wondering whether I'd find any willing participants. I gave out the first of the packs to mums dropping their children off and explained about my research. I needn't have worried about whether there would be any takers, because as soon as people could see I was giving away free bags of 'goodies' they started to approach me, offering to help with the research too. All in all, most were pretty interested and willing to help. I did have the occasional person decline, which was a little disappointing given that they were in my son's class, but I didn't take it personally, as research is not everyone's cup of tea.

In addition to mums at the school gates, I asked the vicar at my local church to help me out. The vicar was so kind, and made an announcement at the end of the church service that anyone interested in helping me with my research could chat to me after the service in the foyer. After the service, I had so many kind people approach me to offer their help as I stood in the corridor with my sample bags. I simply asked them to try the bars with their families and bring back their completed questionnaires the following week.

I also asked, friends, friends of friends, family and anyone else I could find at the time to participate. I gave them products sample bags and questionnaires to pass on within their own circles and spheres of influence. This meant that the reach of my research extended way beyond my community and made it to other parts of the country enabling me to reach hundreds. This also increased the objectivity of my research.

All of the people who took part did so out of their own free will and followed the instructions in the packs to the letter.

WHAT I LEARNED FROM MY LARGER SCALE RESEARCH

I got vital feedback, which I was able to use to improve my product offering, marketing and pitch. People were honest and upfront including all the negatives as well as positives. For example, a few people hated the taste of my fruit bars. Thankfully these were the minority. I noticed that for every 10 people, two absolutely hated the taste, two were average or indifferent and six people really loved the taste. I consoled myself with the knowledge that many hugely successful products have people that either love them or hate them. Marmite is a case in point. The manufacturers of Marmite have used this polarising effect to good effect in their marketing campaigns, celebrating the fact that "you either love it or hate it".

Although some people would clearly never buy my products, I deduced from the questionnaire results that 60% of my respondents would buy my fruit bars if launched on taste alone. Scaling this up to the British population encouraged me to realise that there was a huge market to play for.

Analysing my results also helped me to determine which three flavours of the seven possible varieties I'd included in the packs were preferred. I was able to further narrow this down to the flavours that women and children really liked while paying less attention to the adult male taste preferences, because my main target audience was mums and their children: buying the product for children's lunchboxes and their' handbags as a healthy treat.

CHAPTER 5

HOW TO UNDERSTAND THE BIGGER PICTURE: MARKET TRENDS

"THE ELEPHANT IS LIKE A ROPE"

THE ELEPHANT IS LIKE A ROPE

The story of the blind men and the elephant has been around for generations. Three blind men were asked what an elephant was like. The first blind man, who felt only the elephant's leg, reported that the elephant was like a tree trunk. The second blind man, who felt only the tail, recounted that the elephant was like a rope, while the third blind man, having only felt the elephant's side, concluded that the elephant was like a wall. While each of the blind men was right in describing his experience of an elephant, they did not have the overall picture because each focused on just one part of the animal.

In addition to understanding your target consumer, you need the helicopter view, i.e. an understanding of the marketplace in which your consumer is operating. Researching the overarching trends in your market will give you the wider context you need and help you to obtain the bigger picture.

HOW TO UNDERSTAND THE BIGGER PICTURE: MARKET TRENDS

Market trends are evolving daily. It is essential to be aware of the trends in your chosen market as they happen, and also monitor where they're heading. For example, the ease with which people travel has been helped by the revolution in budget airlines. This has resulted in more people being exposed to international cuisine, flavours and textures more than ever before impacting the personal choices they make when back home.

> *Crisps go international:* 20 years ago the standard crisp flavours were typically salt and vinegar, cheese and onion and ready salted. Since then this market has mushroomed to include even more varieties and flavours. Moreover the crisp market has been refreshed by enterprising smaller businesses introducing new processes such as kettle and pan frying to create crunchy textures. Bag sizes have increased to now encompass our 'eating on the go lifestyles'. There has also been a move towards premium brands springing up with more natural flavours such as sea salt and crushed black pepper. If you were entering the crisp market now an understanding of global trends would help you to anticipate, prepare for and lead the future?

In the cake market there has been a revival in cupcakes, popularised by TV chefs and the media. But if you're moving into cakes now, how could you leverage future trends? At the moment there is so much emphasis on looking beautiful: could your cupcakes have added ingredients that boost skin radiance? This is quite common in Japan right now, where everyday foods are being augmented with additional vitamins and nutrients to boost cosmetic appearance.

Trends are happening everywhere and affect every industry. What are the trends affecting your products and services? Where is your market heading? Could you capitalise on your knowledge of these trends? Could you look to the bigger picture for opportunities to improve your products and services, and create new ones?

By creating unique selling propositions in line with trends, you create a growing desire and market for your goods. You differentiate yourself from your competitors and also increase your chances of getting onto the retailers' shelves. This is because, retailers are not looking for 'copycat' or 'me too' products that simply duplicate what they already have. Because shelf space is limited, retailers are looking for products that will enhance their existing ranges. When they add your products to their shelves, they want your products to bring in new customers rather than just stealing customers away from their existing products which doesn't benefit them: Shifting sales from one product to another may result in growth for you, but zero growth for them.

HOW TO IDENTIFY MARKET TRENDS

While there are a large number of companies that charge significant amounts for information on market trends, it is possible to gain an understanding of the trends in your market for free by gathering information from a range of readily available sources. For example you could:

→ *Read market trend reports*
→ *Have discussions with experts*
→ *Make your own observations*

If you're passionate about your product or service, the research becomes enjoyable.

READ MARKET TREND REPORTS

Visit the larger libraries' business reference sections to gain free access to more formal market reports. The British Library has a whole centre dedicated to business which is free to attend. It is called The British Library Business and IP

Centre and contains a whole host of business reports. Your local city or university library is likely to have the same kind of information. Spend time there asking the librarians how best to access the latest reports for your specific product or service. They will be able to help you to navigate your way through trend information, market size information, growth potential for any given subject or related subject. Familiarise yourself with this information. It will help you to position yourself for sustainable growth and also demonstrate to your potential investors, clients and customers that you know your market inside out.

Read everything else related to your industry. As well as formal market trend reports you can keep aware of trends and topics in your area by looking at a range of media including magazines, trade journals, newspapers and the internet. Libraries are a good source of these on all sorts of industry, both for consumers and practitioners helping you to . From these, acquire a wealth of information. Your bedtime reading will never be the same again.

DISCUSSIONS WITH EXPERTS

As well as checking out market trend reports, join specific interest groups, and forums either in person (see advice on networking in chapter 2) or online, for example on social media sites. Doing this will enable you to ask questions from experts and keep abreast of the latest conversations. You can also help out others by answering their questions and joining in the debate.

For example, if you are a beauty therapist, why not join some meet-up groups in person, or sign up online to free interest groups, blogs and social media sites? These will get you involved in the conversation in terms of what people are trialling, what their results are and what new techniques they are using.

The great thing about social media is that conversations are evolving at break-neck speed with new knowledge added continuously. The conversation on social media platforms is rich, because people from all around the world participate. If you can't find a group relevant to your product or service, you can always start your own group. These are free to create on most social media platforms including *Facebook* and *LinkedIn*.

HOW TO MAKE YOUR OWN OBSERVATIONS: UNDERSTAND YOUR PURCHASING ENVIRONMENT

The best way to understand your purchase environment is to get out there and observe. Watch what's going on with your potential consumers. How are they purchasing? (Do they read the labels, are they impulsive, what is that gets them to take that product of the shelf or click the buy button?) Where do your consumers purchase? Is that at the shops, in the markets, at the gym, online?

The type of purchasing environment in which your consumers access your products and services will vary according to your business model. For example, it may be online, on the high street, in the supermarkets, beauty parlours, gyms, farmers' markets or anywhere else you aim to sell your products, or a combination of these.

Whichever type of outlet you are aiming for, the key is to understand it. When there, check out your competitors. All of this will help you to firm up your 'Unique Selling Points' (USP's).

The following exercise will help you to understand your purchase environment. The principles in the exercise can be adapted to any purchase environment and help you assess your main distribution channel.

EXERCISE 4: **HOW TO UNDERSTAND THE PURCHASING ENVIRONMENT**

1. *Visit the store environment (often known as a store check) or the type of place where you anticipate the majority of your sales will take place.*

2. *When you are inside the store, find out where products similar to the one you are going to launch are located. This may sound simple, but often it's more complicated. For example, if your product is a snack bar, you might find most snack bars close to the checkout. However, on closer inspection, you will find snack bars in the cereal bars section, the biscuits aisle, the world foods section, the health section, the free from additives section of the store and so forth.*

3. *Review the assortment of products in each section of the store. Find out which brands make up the range.*

   - *What is their packaging like?*
   - *Do any particular brands stand out on the shelf and scream "Buy me"?*
   - *What are the differences between the products being offered?*
   - *Why should the retailer stock your product and why should the consumer buy yours above what's already there?*
   - *Is your product going to be better than what you are seeing on the shelf? If so, in what ways? Make a note of them.*

4. *In relation to your own products ask yourself:*

   - *Do you have an edge over what you see on the shelf?*

– Are your ingredients more premium?

– Do you have more interesting features, designs, ingredients or processes than what is being currently offered?

– Are your prices going to be lower, higher or on par?

– Are your USPs strong enough to give the outlet a reason to stock your products?

This knowledge is vital because when it comes to pitching to the outlet you have identified, you will need to prove that your product is going to add value to their product range. You want to be sure that you are creating products that consumers want to and will buy. The above exercise will help you to clarify whether your product has an edge and will not just be the next 'copycat' or 'me too' product.

HOW TO SCRUTINISE YOUR COMPETITORS' PRODUCTS

Find out what your unique selling points are for your product, i.e. what makes your product or service, different to those already in the supermarkets, high street or on the web. What makes your service better than that which is already on the market? To understand this and be able to draw customers' attention to the best things about your product you need to develop a good understanding of what's already being done.

How does my product measure up? Taking the snack bar example from above, how many calories will your product contain versus other bars? If yours has considerably fewer, could this be your USP? Consumers are becoming increasingly conscious of weight issues. Alternatively, does your bar have more natural ingredients than other bars on the market?

Consumers are always looking for simpler ingredients: could this be your USP? Does your bar simply taste better? Find out what the other bars taste like. Even better, ask your focus group to give you their honest opinion on how your bar tastes versus the competition. The words they use to describe your product as against the competition can result in some powerful descriptions which you can use to pitch to the retailer and also pitch to your potential customers in your marketing materials.

HOW TO FIND THE GAPS!

If there is anything missing from a retailer's range, your product could be just what they are looking for. It's therefore important that you find these gaps and use them to build your sales proposition to the retailer. Retailers need to know that your product is not just a 'me too' or 'copycat' product similar to what they already stock. Therefore, if you fully understand their range, you can point out why your product will add value to them. This might be the fact they your product has superior features, ingredients, portion size, benefits, etc., versus what the retailer already has. However, until you find the gaps you will not be able to demonstrate this.

MY STORY

I wanted to understand the bigger picture and the wider trends happening in my industry. I approached some of the major data gathering organisations in order to obtain data on my market but found their service charges were in the thousands of pounds and their reports were equally pricey. Having contacted several 'data houses' I realised that the majority were geared up to service large corporate organisations and had totally overlooked the needs of entrepreneurs and start-up level businesses. Not having the funds to support the high prices charged by the data houses, I thoroughly researched the trends happening myself at low to zero-cost.

In particular, I extracted my information from a range of sources including libraries, the media at large, discussions with experts, my own personal observations, as well as attending seminars, trade shows and generally getting out and about.

WHAT I LEARNED

When I looked at the 'macro' or large scale trends affecting the UK in the area of food I found several that strengthened the reasons for launching my fruit bars. For example, the obesity crisis was frequently being reported in the market trend reports, newspapers, television and media at large. To address this, the government was running campaigns aimed at encouraging consumers to eat more healthily by introducing at least five fruit and vegetable portions into the diet - the 'Five a day' campaign.

Given the obesity epidemic, I felt that introducing my fruit bars would be timely because they would make a positive contribution to healthy eating. One of my fruit bars was equivalent to one portion of fruit so counted as one of 'the five a day'.

Other trends happening in the nation was the move to remove hidden salt from foods and the encouragement to reduce salt intake to less than 6g a day per person.

Again, the fact that my fruit bars had no added salt meant that they compared well in comparison to a number of salt-laden snacks in the aisles.

Market reports that I'd read from reference libraries showed that the market for healthier style snacks such as fruit bars was rising significantly, albeit from a small base. These reports showed how consumers were making a conscious effort to move away from artificial ingredients and artificial additives in food that they know can be harmful. This was reflected in the insight I'd gained from my focus groups.

All of the trends and information I discovered from analysing market trends through, library reports, the internet, and discussions with experts, in-store, and competitor reviews, all confirmed to me that launching the fruit bar was the right thing to do.

My main challenge became how to launch my fruit bar in a format that mums and children alike would want to buy. The format from overseas clearly wouldn't work and needed a significant redesign. The next chapter shares how I achieved the look and feel of product that consumers wanted to buy.

CHAPTER 6

HOW TO DEVELOP
YOUR BRAND

"STAND OUT FROM THE CROWD"

BRANDING: WHY YOU SHOULD DO IT AND
WHO SHOULD DO IT FOR YOU

It's important to develop a brand identity that your customers will connect with. The brand you ultimately create will be one that your customers learn to associate with you and your product or service. It should engender confidence in the consumer and also set your product or service apart from the competition. For this reason it's important to get your brand identity spot on for your range. For this reason, I would recommend using a professional.

How do I choose the right agency for me? There are hundreds of companies that specialise in creating brand identity. A simple internet search of brand agencies will come up with lists of branding and design companies that you can approach to help you come up with your brand and design.

Be sure to look for companies that have a track record of designing in your field. For example, food branding design experts will have a totally different look and feel to those that design for other services. The colour palettes and styling used, for example, may be entirely different. With hygiene products such as shampoo, palettes are normally cool blues and clinical whites, for example while a brand design agency specialising in food will be used to using warmer tones which have inherent food associations.

The two types of project are entirely different and engage consumers in different types of purchase behaviour. Therefore where possible select the right design company with bags of experience in your chosen field or product type. The great thing about using the internet to find branding and design companies is that you can view their work online. They often have examples of their client work on their websites.

If you prefer working on paper, the business reference sections in larger libraries contain compendiums and directories of branding agencies which will help you to compile a shortlist of agencies to contact. Whether you choose to search for design agencies on the web or via directories in the library, there are plenty to choose from, so you will need to create a shortlist of those design/branding agencies that you feel will definitely be able to understand your product.

In your shortlist choose those designers that will have an affinity with what you're trying to achieve. Their work history should speak for itself. If you don't like what they have done for other people then it's likely that you are not going to like what will do for you so move on swiftly. When making a shortlist of companies to choose from, don't be afraid to go for the 'big players'. By big players, I mean those designers and brand agencies that design for well-known worldwide brands, are best in class and are at the top of their game. It is possible to engage such companies, even on a low budget. I know it's possible because I managed to secure a top London design and branding agency to develop my brand with a very limited budget indeed, and I share how I achieved that later, in the *my story* section of this chapter.

Once you have your shortlist of 20 or so design companies, start to contact them. Explain your project over the phone and gauge their interest. Book a meeting with those that you feel you can work with in order to discuss your project further. You will invariably get some agencies that will say "no thank you" to a meeting to discuss your project further. Some companies will tell you that they are too busy to take on your project, and others simply won't want to work on a shoestring budget.

Don't be put off by this, just keep working through your shortlist. Don't be put off by some of their stipulations or high prices, either. Negotiations can always take place later down the line and deals can always be done once you get into a dialogue with the decision makers. From your shortlist of 20 you should aim to meet up with around 6. Any more and it starts to get confusing.

Meeting the agency: Where should I do it? In terms of the location of the meeting that you set up, you need to be professional. You could either go to their offices for the appointment, or even better and cheaper still, get them to come to your neck of the woods or as close to you as possible. I suggest using the lobby of a local hotel that's convenient to you or at least a half-way point between you and them. You won't have to pay for using the hotel lounge or lobby, and in fact you'll find many business meetings going on at the same time as yours.

If possible, go out beforehand and familiarise yourself with your local hotel and their layout in order to pick the best one for the meeting. Check out, for example, whether there are plugs you can use for your laptop situated conveniently next to a quiet corner table. This is so that if you want to show your prospective designers a presentation or photos of your products and ideas, you can do so with minimal interruption and without the worry of your laptop battery running down. Scope out where you will sit and the prices of teas and coffees and coffees so that when you leave you won't get a shock.

HOW TO PREPARE FOR YOUR MEETING
WITH THE DESIGNERS

It's particularly helpful to be able to communicate your project really well, sharing any thoughts you may have for branding and design. In particular, it would be helpful to explain at your initial meeting what your vision is for your product or service, where you'd like to see it sold, and who you envisage using or consuming it, because the person who buys a product doesn't necessarily use it but may be buying it for other members of their household. So have this ready in advance. It's a good idea to note this down, or use slides, and also to take actual samples of your wares with you.

It is also useful to share an overview of the results of any research you've conducted, such as focus groups, questionnaires and discussions with various interested parties, and what you think your unique product selling points are. This information you provide will give the design agency a great start in understanding your product and target consumer. The more understanding the design agency has, the more informed their proposals will be in relation to your product or service. Your information will also help them to know who best within their team to assign to your project.

Meeting the Agency: What should I ask? During your meeting, ask the design/branding agency how they like to work and what their process is for dealing with start-up products. Other questions to raise may include whether you will have your own dedicated person to liaise with. Does the agency have a long or short turnaround time for their output? Finding out as much information as you can will help you to decide which agency you are most comfortable working with.

BIG DESIGNERS DO TAKE ON SMALL PROJECTS

When you explain your ideas to the design houses, do so with so much enthusiasm that they will want to work with you. You want them to be as excited as you are about your products. This way, when they start talking prices, you will be in a position of strength, because you have convinced them that your product or service is going to become the next best thing since sliced bread, and they will not want to miss out on getting on board early. You really can do this.

More importantly, you'll need to explain the limitations of your budget. You'll be surprised at how much some of the agencies will reduce their prices. This might not happen straight away: it may become an iterative discussion involving them having to consult internally with their organisations and get back to you. Remember that during a recession they are likely to welcome your business, even if it's small. If you communicate potential for growth in your brand and that this project is likely to gather momentum and generate money going forward, they may be willing to take it on that basis, and charge you minimal fees.

How to give them a win-win situation: A designer may take on your project at preferential rates because they would like to develop internal talent. Often many of the large scale brands they currently work on are not exercising the latent design skills of their team because of the restrictions placed on them. For example, try changing the Apple brand design, Cadbury's colour purple, or Nike's iconic tick. No design team would dare to deviate from the sacred on such brands and so they are raring to put their creativity to work on new upcoming fresh projects. Yours could be just what they are looking for, in which case you have a win-win scenario. You allow the designers to unleash their creative potential while they give you an amazing product that's fresh, exciting and very 'on trend' and customer focused.

The more you practise and prepare at home before the meeting, the better. Practise in front of an audience. Get used to expressing your enthusiasm for your own brand.

NEXT STEPS

At the end of the meeting ask what the next steps will be for both parties, for example, when will the agency come back to you with their proposals. The meeting should end with dates or a promise of dates for when the agency will come back to you. Of course, if neither company is interested from what they've heard, then politely thank them and move on to the next one.

It is a good idea to get all of the designers to come back for the next meeting with their proposals on a certain date or across a couple of dates that are close together, so that you remain concentrated on that task and can assess the merits of each proposal while they are still fresh in your mind. On the day of the proposal, the design company will give you an outline of ideas they envisage for your brand, and what it will cost you to go forward. If you like what you see then haggle down the price like mad.

TOP TIPS: **WORKING WITH BRAND DESIGN AGENCIES**

1. *Use a professional service where possible to help you to create your brand. Your brand should communicate the essence of your products, service or business, so needs to be robust.*

2. *Compile a shortlist of brand design companies which have expertise in your chosen field. You can use the internet to do this or alternatively use the compendiums held within large libraries.*

---

3. *Don't be afraid of targeting some of the larger companies.*

4. *Prepare well in advance for all of your meetings in order to get the most out of them. Be prepared to share information about your target audience, marketplace and aspirations for your products and services.*

5. *Don't be afraid to haggle on price.*

6. *Ensure that you end each meeting with mutually agreed next steps and dates for further meetings.*

MY STORY

Feedback from my focus groups confirmed that I had a great tasting product but raised the matter of poor packaging. The focus group comments on my product packaging were so negative that I knew I needed a major overhaul and to do this would require the help of professional packaging designers. However, I also knew that as well as create some fab looking products, I needed to create a brand that consumers could connect with. In my long-term plan, I envisaged creating a whole range of products that would extend beyond fruit bars. I needed to have a brand that could be rolled out to different categories. I was essentially thinking growth.

Even though the initial launch of my product range would consist of a small range of fruit bars, I believed that my brand would grow and branch out into other fruit-related products such as fruit jam and fruit tea. I envisaged that in the future, my product range would become more than fruit bars and included this thinking both the goals I set and the plans I made to achieve those goals. I used my goals and vision to inspire me to progress and to determine the direction of that progress.

HOW I SEARCHED

I searched the internet for design companies that specialized in branding creation. I specifically used the terms 'design and branding' rather than just design alone because I wanted to create a robust brand and not just pretty designs. This was important to me given my vision and goals.

I found searching for the design and branding agencies on the internet a really enjoyable process as it enabled me to, see examples of their work online and assess their suitability for my project.

From several, I earmarked around 20 that I felt could do a really good job on the basis of their area of expertise, their ethos and their design quality. Most of had expertise in the food industry, so were used to working with food products understanding how consumers make food choices and what was required to capture attention in the aisles.

In addition to their brand design credentials and examples of their work, I also included location among my criteria. Being based in London myself, I sought companies in London and also within a 20 mile radius. I felt that anything further would have limited my physical interactions and I was keen to meet the people who were going to take my project forward. I saw my project as my 'baby' and wanted to be as close to the developments as possible.

I began phoning the 20 companies on my shortlist. I introduced myself and explained that I had a design project that I'd like to discuss. I then mentioned my limited budget. It was at this point that the process momentarily ceased to be enjoyable. The first, then the second, then the third, then the fourth company I rang all said that they were not able to work within the confines of that budget and quickly ended the dialogue, wishing me success in my endeavour to find an agency that would work within the confines of my budget.

When this happened several times in a row I started to feel a little discouraged, as if there was no design company on earth that could work within my confines. However, I kept going, fuelled by my mum's words, instilled into me from as far back as I can remember: "If at first you don't succeed, try, try, try again". And so I did. Through persistence, I found six companies that were willing to come to the table. To my amazement, three of them were what I'd call design 'giants', and three were smaller innovative companies, all with great merits.

I eagerly fixed dates in the diary with these six companies, choosing the lobby of a fine local hotel as a meeting place. As with most major hotels chains, this was free to use, quiet and professional. I'd found a great spot with close access to a plug surrounded by comfy sofas. This location became my own personal office for the day, ordering coffee from what felt like my own personal waitress. Perfect! I spread my six agency appointments over 3 days at this hotel.

HOW I PREPARED

In the time leading up to my first face-to-face meetings with the design/branding agencies, I gathered together all I knew about my fruit bars:

→ *I made a bullet point list of the all the benefits and USPs of the bars because I wanted the design houses to be able to communicate these benefits in their designs.*

→ *I created a summary of my focus group results.*

→ *As well as the good things, I included the things that my target group disliked about the original packaging for my fruit bars I certainly didn't want the new design company to repeat any of the old mistakes!*

→ *I included the fact that people wanted to see recycling instructions on the packaging, they wanted cardboard (not the flimsy plastic that currently housed my bars), and many other discoveries.*

→ *I summarised what I felt was going on in terms of market trends and my competitors.*

MY PITCH TO THEM

The day of my first meeting arrived. It was with one of the larger companies. To my surprise, they sent one of their directors and a project manager to meet me. It felt amazing to be speaking to such high calibre designers who were considering my project seriously. I struggled contain my joy at what felt like such design 'royalty' coming to see me, about my project and right round the corner from my house!

Of course, I maintained my professional composure: "Thank you for taking the time out to meet with me. I propose we proceed as follows..." I outlined how I envisaged how our meeting should go. I then asked them to provide some background about the way they worked and asked some questions about how they would ensure my project, which was considerably smaller to those they were used to working on, would not be lost among their bigger clients, as this was a concern of mine. They were quick to reassure me that they would allocate a project manager to me and I would be kept at the forefront of progress, and be consulted regularly on key decisions. Music to my ears!

I then proceeded to describe my project with great enthusiasm, using the slides I'd prepared on my laptop. I was in glorious full flow, passionately communicating that my fruit bars were going to be the next big trend to sweep the nation, given the perfect timing market trends, the fact that people loved the taste and had indicated in my research their desire to purchase. To prove how good my bars tasted I gave them samples to taste.

The director and project manager were impressed with the taste of the fruit bars and the clarity of the information I'd communicated. We concluded that they would go away and put together a pitch which would take about 4 weeks to prepare. At the pitch they would give me some idea of how they would propose taking the project forward in the light of the information

I'd supplied. They also offered to pick up the tab for the copious amounts of coffee and biscuits that I'd ordered during the meeting.

Over the next three days I met with the other design companies in my self-styled 'office' of this fine Hotel lounge. My meetings were supercharged with energy as I passionately explained my product, thoughts and ideas and quizzed the design companies on their various protocols. Each agency agreed that they would come up with proposals and would pitch for my business, even though I had such a small budget! A few of the agencies said that they could not provide any visual proposals, as this was not best industry practice, but others were more than happy to provide visuals.

THEIR PROPOSALS (PITCH) BACK TO ME

The date was set for each agency to pitch their ideas back to me. In terms of venue, this time round, I hired a meeting room in another local hotel which had a good deal on offer. I felt the need to hire a room because this time round, we were past our initial introductory discussion and closer to serious business. Some of the agencies had mentioned that they would be bringing more of their people as well as large visual boards and presentations. The meeting room was ideal for all of this because it had a large screen and a projector, all included in the price. Interestingly, the agencies asked whether they needed to bring their own projector and screen, so even if the hotel hadn't laid them on, the agencies would have come fully equipped.

On The pitch day I felt a little bit like a judge on a popular TV talent show, given the privilege of judging the designers' proposals. I sat excitedly, keen to see how each agency would take my project forward. I scrutinised the brightly coloured vision boards presented by each agent as they described how their visual ideas could relate to my brand.

Some of the ideas presented to me by the design agencies I can only describe as being way out there. Like the designer that presented a cartoon picture of an enormous hippopotamus with a rather large rear stomping around splattering fruit all over the place. Not quite what I'd envisaged for my sophisticated fruit bars. It took a great deal of restraint to hold my composure when all I wanted to do was yell at the top of my voice, "Nooo!"

My parents had always brought me up with the notion that if you can't say anything nice then don't say anything at all. What could I say at this point, as the designer asked for my feedback? "Wow," I said, then paused. "This is a really imaginative interpretation of the brief". The designer smiled, to my relief, and I quickly moved the conversation on. The next two design houses presented images that were pretty credible but not really memorable. The fourth design house presented images that seemed a little too familiar, as if they'd taken the bestselling snack bar on the market to all intents and purposes copied it. It was too close for comfort. I didn't think design agencies could get away with that, but you learn something new every day.

The fifth brand creation agency was quite intriguing. They didn't show any concepts visually because they said that this was not protocol and would breach their design code guidelines. However, they did describe in schematic detail the process that they would undertake to fulfil my project.

Company number six also didn't present any visual concepts that they had worked on, but instead to chose to show a 'story board' of items that they would use to take their inspiration from to demonstrate their understanding of my aspirations for the project.

There was so much information to take in from the six companies and some of it was quite mind boggling. Three companies would have been enough.

HOW I CHOSE MY DESIGN AGENCY

I made the decision to go with agency number five. I was a little sceptical at first, because they refused to show visuals but instead spent their time explaining their internal procedures and how they would treat my project. I was convinced that by following their procedure in the amount of detail they presented, eventually we would achieve a desirable outcome in terms of brand and product design.

However, this agency was the most expensive and was requesting fees that I just couldn't afford. Although I haggled to get the price down, they were just not budging. In the end, I asked whether I could pay them in instalments on a listings basis. For example, they would gain money for each retailer I secured with the new designs that they had vowed to create. This way, their payment would be performance based. I would only pay them each time I landed a major retail client. They agreed. Phew! Both parties were tied in to each other's success and a classic win-win scenario was created.

HOW WE ACHIEVED A 'WIN-WIN'

One of the reasons the design agency agreed to my proposal was this: they were used to dealing with major companies whose designs were sacrosanct. To change the iconic designs of their existing customers would have been sacrilege, so as designers their creative talents were being limited to sprucing up designs rather than creating new ones. Their young design talent were being stifled by not having projects to work on from scratch where they could flex their creative muscles and awaken their imagination.

The director felt that my project offered a great opportunity for her young design talent to get stuck into and experiment with new techniques. For me, the deal gave me the opportunity to work with a top design agency with no cash changing hands up front. Payment would be required, not on job completion but, even better, when I'd secured supermarket shelf space and could afford it.

I had confidence that the design company I chose would treat my project professionally and would also prioritise its development, given that they would want to get their investment back as soon as possible, and allow me to start selling into the supermarkets and on the internet at the earliest opportunity. I was assured they would do their best because they would want me to get into the supermarkets in order to recoup their investment, so needed to create brilliant designs.

TO AND FRO

Once I had agreed to use the fifth design agency, their legal team put together a contract outlining that for every retailer that I secured as an outlet for my fruit bars, I would pay them an agreed proportion of their fee. For a large retailer listing, I would give the design agency a proportionately larger amount, and when a smaller retailer listed the products, I would pay a smaller amount to the designers. The payments had a ceiling, up to the value of the original fee they had quoted.

Contract details: The good thing about the payments was that the contract was stacked in my favour. I was allowed to delay payment until each supermarket chain agreed to stock my products. Furthermore, I was granted a 60 day period of time from going on shelf to paying the agency number five. Finally, the last part of the deal which favoured me was the caveat for the number of stores within a retailer listing. So for example if only 20% of a large chains stores stocked the product, I would only be due to pay the designer 20% of the agreed listing payment for that retailer after 60 days, i.e. when I'd received payment from the retailer. This was such a valuable agreement for me because it meant that I did not need to get out a hefty loan or second mortgage in order to pay design fees. It also meant that if the project failed and I got no listings at all, I would not have to pay anything to the agency. So I would be walking away debt free.

WORK BEGINS

Work on my fruit bar brand creation project began as soon as I'd signed the contract. I regularly attended meetings at the design team's offices to review progress. Having chosen a London agency so close to my home meant that the journey was quick, easy and relatively low cost. I looked forward to every meeting with my designer. In our first meeting, the designer showed me a range of concept boards depicting how my fruit bars might look with a new packaging format, i.e. a box rather than a bag. The concept boards also showed various brand name ideas. Three of the names and straplines that the agency had come up with stood out as being likely heroes but rather than make an on the spot decision, I decided to take the concept boards away to think further on the matter before making my decision.

In particular, I wanted to garner the opinion of those who mattered most, my target audience. The only problem was that I needed to do so quite quickly and at little or no cost. Again, avoiding the use of large costly market research agencies, I thought of ways to canvass more mums. Bingo: my son, Benjamin, had been invited to his friend's birthday party at the local children's indoor play area. I knew that there would be several mums sitting twiddling their thumbs at the party waiting for their children, and because Ben's friend went to a different school, they would use cast fresh eyes on my project. I asked permission from Ben's friend's mum if I could bring my concept boards to the parents waiting area of the party, and she kindly agreed.

THANK GOD FOR CHILDREN'S PARTIES

So there I was, at a children's party, in the parents' waiting area, showing a group of mums my concept boards and engaging in lively discussion with them about the merits and demerits of the three separate brand names. Some of them were intrigued, about what I was trying to achieve and were really happy to help, as it was an interesting way to pass the time. Many of them said how brave I was for trying to launch my own brands and succeed in business. It made me feel on top of the world to have the support, encouragement and kind words of other mums. It gave me a much needed boost to know that other people were interested in what I was doing and were more than happy to give their feedback.

At the end of the party, I had a pretty good idea of which brand name was proving most popular with the mums and the reasons why. Furthermore, many of them had enjoyed the research so much that they offered to help with any further ideas that I wanted to test!

As well as the feedback from the birthday party, I sought further feedback from other people, including my family, and children, because children were ultimately going to be key consumers of my fruit bars. The decision was almost unanimous regarding what the brand name should be. Both mums and children liked the brand name for my fruit bars because it conveyed a concept of a lifestyle. Some felt that the name implied that you should eat more fruit, which was a clear association with the fruit bar as a product. Others liked the name because it was fun, sounded upbeat, and was easy to remember. As well as being liked by target audience, the brand name was brilliant for strategic purposes because it could be used as an 'umbrella' brand under which I could launch a whole range of fruit products in the future as my fruit bar business grew.

"ASK FOR THE MOON AND YOU MIGHT JUST GET IT"

I continued to attend developmental meetings with the agency, commenting and providing feedback on every stage of the brand design and development. I asked for product photography on the pack, even though food photography is specialist and costly. Brand agencies often outsource their on-pack photography to professionals, adding significant cost to any given project. This did not deter me from asking for natural fruit photography on the pack because I felt my fruit bars needed to set themselves apart from the competition. The few bars that existed on the market used either cartoon imagery on pack or artist's impressions of fruit. I felt that providing real fruit photography on pack would convey to the consumer the fruit content of the bar and also the premium nature of the fruit bar, because my bars were predominantly fruit (other bars on the market had a lower amount of fruit, even just 10%, but still called themselves fruit bars).

The agency agreed to do the photography because they had an in-house team of designers keen to learn photography techniques. This team had never really been given an opportunity in previous projects because the big companies expect them to outsource and use photography professionals. As it was the design team's first stab at in-house photography, they gave my project the best amount of attention that they could. The design company and I liaised a lot by email too and sent PDFs by email and proofs by courier all for me to approve the text, pictures, styles, etc.

HOW I CONNECTED WITH MY TARGET AUDIENCE

I wrote the words to go on the back of my fruit bar boxes packs myself. It felt more personal this way and I really wanted to connect directly with my customers in a friendly conversational tone which wasn't contrived or gimmicky. I felt that when I wrote the message on the back of the pack I was speaking from one mum to another, remaining true to my brand ethos.

After several meetings with the design agency, and much discussion with mums and their children, my brand name and design were completed. I'd gone from having fruit bars that I'd imported in awkward-looking dark green, plastic packaging, with a name but no real brand identity, to a crisp clean looking design, great brand name, beautiful shelf stand out and environmentally friendly packaging. The cost of the professional designers was worth every penny, or every penny that I would eventually have to pay when my fruit bars went live into stores. I now had a beautifully designed product.

HOW I PRINTED THE PACKAGING

As I was importing my fruit bars, it was more logical to have my fruit bars wrapped in their new packaging as they came off the production line in Scandinavia. The alternative of unpacking and repackaging the bars in England would have been cumbersome and more expensive. I therefore asked the UK design company to send the designs they had created electronically to a Scandinavian print firm who printed all of the packaging and proceeded to send it to my manufacturer. This reduced handling, costs and complexity.

Soon I was on a plane, full of excitement, ready to witness the first print run of my lovely new designs and packaging. At the printers, I beamed with pride as I saw huge rolls of my packaging come off the conveyor belt at great speed.

Final touches: The printers tore a piece off the trial production run for my approval and comments. At that point, I decided the ink on the strawberry variety needed to be a much more vibrant red. The printers were able to adjust the print run there and then so that all subsequent rolls of the packaging were printed in juicy red perfection. I did the same for the orange on the apricot fruit bar and also the mauve on the fig variety, which both needed cranking up slightly to provide deep colour. Once satisfied, I put my signature on each print record to show that I was happy with the colours and designs. Job done.

I left the printers knowing that my fruit bars would soon have all of their wonderful packaging put on them at source and would be in pristine condition when they arrived in the UK. Now all I needed to do was to 'create some noise' about my beautiful finished products.

CHAPTER 7

HOW TO GET INTO THE PRESS AND ONTO THE RADIO

"CREATE SOME NOISE"

INTRODUCTION

If I told you that you could publicise your product, service or business on national television, national radio and national press including magazines and newspapers, all for free, you might not believe me. But this is exactly what I achieved with my natural fruit bar company. The extensive coverage of both my business and products on national radio and in the press were not a result of paid advertising or paid-for PR: I didn't pay a thing. Instead the coverage I achieved was largely the result of creativity and perseverance.

When I set out to launch my products, numerous PR companies and specialists approached me, asking me to pay them in exchange for promoting my business and products through various media. I was quoted 2000 per month for the services of one such company, who said that the charge would be payable irrespective of their success in gaining media attention.

Although I realised the value that great PR companies can leverage, I politely declined their services because like most start-up companies, I simply could not afford to use them. While larger companies rely heavily on marketing and PR companies to help build awareness of their brands, products or services, the fees these PR companies charge are often beyond the reach of new entrepreneurs.

Having decided not to use the services of PR companies, I knew that I still needed some great PR to help launch and promote my brand, business and personal profile. In the absence of cash for a PR budget, I decided to do my own marketing and PR, and learn to do it well. In this chapter, I describe how you, too, can achieve exposure for your own products or service on national radio and press all for free.

YOU HAVE THE KNOWLEDGE

Who better to tell the world about your products than you? You know your products and services inside out, you've understood their development, and you've been keeping up to date on the marketplace. No other person knows as much about your product as you do: you are the expert. Furthermore, because you've worked hard on the development of your products, you're totally passionate about them.

HOW TO GET MAGAZINE COVERAGE FOR FREE

Magazine coverage can be priceless, because you can often reach huge numbers of your target audience. Some weekly magazines have readerships into the hundreds of thousands, so having your story published in them is a successful strategy for getting your message across to wide numbers of your target audience. Of course, you can always take out a paid advertisement but the secret to getting your products featured for free is to create a story that is of interest to the readership.

There are hundreds of magazine titles out there covering every niche from health to home, gadgets, cars, fashion, food, lifestyle, love, and a whole range in between. Every magazine has its own specific target audience in terms of readership, so it's crucial you pick the right magazine with a readership that matches your target audience. Magazine editors, journalists and freelance contributors are all looking for material that will stimulate and interest their readership.

SHARE TOP TIPS AND COMMENT ON TRENDS

You might have some top tips to share that would suit the readership. If you manage to write and place an article sharing your best tips in relation to your industry that your target audience will be interested in, although you may not be able to feature your product directly, you will be credited as the author of the article and will have your contact details printed, including your website. Readers can then check out your products or services if they enjoy what they've read.

If you're passionate about your product or service and you're immersed in the trends leading your market place, chances are you know more than most, even enough to write an informative article that gives readers a heads up on the future and things worth looking out for.

CREATE A STORY

Another good way to gain magazine interest in your product, business or service is to create a story, and to present that story in a way that's appealing to the readership of the magazine you are aiming for. By story, I don't mean fiction. Instead I'm referring to creating an article or 'story' that is true, topical, current, and relevant to the magazine's audience, which positions your product, business or service in the frame. There are so many aspects of your life that will help you to create a magazine-worthy article.

All of us have life experiences that other people would find fascinating if we chose to share them so why not consider sharing those experiences to help/inform other and promote your business at the same time? To appeal to magazines, you will need to position your product or service in an interesting way that captures the reader's attention. Some of the ideas in Exercise 4, may sound a little dramatic but are typical of the stories that make up a large swathe of the 'reader's interest' stories in many magazines. Most of us have experienced ups and downs in life. Writing about these things in the light or what we are achieving in the business or service we provide can really encourage, support and inform others, while having the benefit of introducing your product or service to the wider readership.

NEWSPAPERS

Like magazines, newspapers are always on the lookout for interesting stories that will grab the attention of their readership. The local and regional press try to feature stories about people within their circulation area. The key to securing their interest is to be interesting. They don't simply want you to send them an advert for your business, unless, of course, you are paying for an advert in the classified section, but they really like to hear about topical matters, local success stories and local challenges as it touches the heart of the local community.

RADIO

You can never get enough good publicity for your brand, product or service. Radio coverage is another way to achieve this. The key to gaining radio coverage without paying for it is to create a general interest story that is topical, relevant, on trend and makes you the 'go to' person for that subject matter.

Targeting the right radio station for your coverage is essential. There are hundreds of radio stations, some aimed at sport, music, the arts, discussion and so forth. When you look for radio stations to target, try to gain an idea of the audience for their programmes. Choose programmes that will give you the best publicity to your target market.

EXERCISE 5: HOW TO FIND YOUR PUBLICITY ANGLE

Ask yourself these questions:

→ *Do you have top tips you can share?*

→ *Can you help readers to keep abreast of trends or throw light on the latest craze?*

→ *Are celebrities known to use similar products or services to yours for example in their health or fitness regime? Are they wearing them, or anything similar to what you make? If so you can show how the public can achieve a similar outcome or look.*

→ *Is there a new trend about to sweep the nation, and your product or service is at the forefront?*

→ *Is there a transformational story that you can highlight? For example Has setting up your business, product or service given you better self-esteem or even given you the means to escape from an oppressive relationship?*

→ *Has your product or service made a remarkable difference in your life or the life or anyone you know?*

→ *Did you set up your product or service in the face of adversity and have now triumphed over it?*

→ *Did you set up your product or service because you were frustrated about what was currently on the market? could other readers identify with the same frustrations you initially had and would they find that they could overcome them as you have?*

→ *Have you met a celebrity through your work?*

→ *Have you helped a charity through your work?*

If you answer yes to any of the above questions, you can, use these as a basis to formulate an interesting story to send to magazine editors, journalists and radio stations. These are just some ideas. If none of these apply, why not wrack your brains for interesting scenarios and events you've encountered from your own situations.

HOW TO CONTACT MAGAZINES, NEWSPAPERS AND RADIO JOURNALISTS

Professional PR companies that charge for their services have lists of contacts within the media that comprise editors, journalists, and researchers. Why not compile your own list? In the past, you needed large numbers of connections to get names. Now that so much information is in the public domain, with a little tenacity you can access that information too.

There are a number of ways to contact magazines. For example, an internet search for your chosen magazine title, adding the words 'contact us' should bring up a list of contacts for that particular title ranging from editor to the head of each section featured within the magazine. Here you may also find phone numbers and emails.

Depending on the magazine title, rather than a list of names and numbers which is helpful, you may simply end up with a 'contact us' enquiry box to which you can request the contact details of the best person to deal with your proposal.

When submitting your synopsis, try to send it to the editor or journalist for the section of the magazine that fits your angle or story best. For example is it the 'Real life' stories section, or is it the section on lifestyles, new gadgets or health and career matters? Find out who is the key contact person for your chosen section.

You can also conduct an internet search of freelance writers and journalists. Once you look at their profile you will see the types of story that they generally cover and the types of press they write for. You can use this information to select which freelancers are most likely to take up your story.

If computers are not your thing, pick up a copy of the magazine or publication you are interested in targeting, from the library or a local shop and scour the pages. In magazines, the front contents page normally lists the contact list of contributors and how to contact them, while for newspapers, the names of the contributors typically come at the end of each article or head up each section.

RADIO

Many radio stations are similar to magazines in their reporting and programming. They have slots for business, the arts, entertainment, music, sports, women etc. Choose your slots carefully, contacting the researcher of the programme relevant to your product idea or business. For example if your business is centred around children, choose a programme targeted specifically at mums with children and contact the researcher associated with that programme. Programme contact details can be found on the internet.

> **SIGN UP FOR THE NEWSLETTERS ON
> 'ASPIRING ACTOR' WEBSITES**

This may sound a little crazy, especially if you are not an aspiring actor however, in addition to acting roles, these websites regularly display requests from freelance writers and journalists looking for interesting stories on behalf of a range of magazine and press titles including the big ones. These requests are typically entitled, "Real life stories wanted for national magazines". You might even end up being paid for your story if it is interesting enough and fits their criteria, as well as benefitting from the publicity and exposure to your target audience.

MY STORY

As a new business start-up, I knew I needed as much exposure within the media as possible to ensure that my target audience found out about my fruit bars. As my start-up funds were limited, I could not afford the fees of PR companies to generate awareness on my behalf. I therefore vowed to gain as much media coverage on my own as I could.

MAGAZINES AND NEWSPAPERS

I carefully selected the magazines that were read by my target audience. Parenting style magazines, women oriented magazines, lifestyle oriented magazines, health magazines and business focussed magazines were all a really good fit for the coverage I was aiming to achieve.

I contacted the editors, journalists and researchers of these magazines by email having searched on both the internet and within the magazines themselves for relevant names. Within my email, I introduced myself and included; a short synopsis of my story idea, why I felt it to be relevant to their readers as well as my contact details.

ONE STORY – A MYRIAD OF ANGLES

I made my story relevant to each type of magazine by highlighting different aspects of it. For example:

→ *For the health and lifestyle magazine, my story focussed on the healthy aspects of my products as an easier way to get five a day given our increasingly busy lifestyles.*

→ *For the parenting magazines, I documented the challenges related to starting-up a business and juggling children at the same time.*

→ *For the business magazines, I focussed on my experience of being made redundant, the economic climate and starting a business in a recession. This was pretty topical to the readership given the significant numbers of people also being made redundant and/or anxious about their future.*

Was it worth it? Yes. I'd put my heart on the line by writing about the rollercoaster ride of emotions I'd experienced during challenging and vulnerable times in my life such as redundancy, starting a business, juggling my family but I hoped that in doing so, I was able to encourage and inspire others going through difficult periods too.. For me, I'd experienced a double benefit of helping people while also letting people know about my wonderful fruit bars, a genuine 'win-win'.

In addition to magazines, I approached the newspapers who featured my story's several times over because of their topical nature. As well as local press, I approached regional and national press alike as well as specific industry journals. Some of the local press ran my stories not only one edition of their paper but across their titles in other boroughs as well. My articles achieved not just a few sentences, but significant spreads.

I reached over a million people through magazines and newspapers and paid nothing for such favourable coverage.

NATIONAL AND LOCAL RADIO STATIONS

I felt that business programmes, lifestyle programmes and women-focused programmes would be ideal for both my personal profile and brand building, as these would reach my target audience and represented the genres that I felt most comfortable with. I also felt that these types of radio programme would be receptive to my story and the aspects of it that I wanted to share.

I wrote with a passion to the programme presenters and researchers of popular radio stations - with the smaller stations these often happened to be the same person. I targeted both large and small stations. I didn't pay a thing, just good old fashioned elbow grease. After a few weeks of zero replies, I secured a slot on the Women's Hour of a national radio station.

How did I get my foot in the door? My email to that radio presenter was simple, to the point and appeared to be a win-win situation. In the email, I introduced myself, explained I was a regular listener who loved the programme and that I felt that my story would interest readers. I outlined in brief how I started my business in the midst of the economic recession. This was quite topical at the time I wrote the email, with daily headlines in the news relaying the numerous businesses that were going bust. I mentioned that I was happy to come to the studio at their convenience and even offered a few dates indicating my availability. That was the short email. Within the body of that email, I included links to other information about me so that if the presenter was interested they could check out my credentials further.

Within a few days of sending that email I had an invitation to appear as the main guest for the women's hour that morning. Excitedly, I prepared by thinking through my story and also looked at current statistics about what was happening in the news. I did this so that I could demonstrate a wider perspective and knowledge about the things affecting the economy as whole and not just me. During the interview, as well as asking me about why I'd dared to start a business in the recession, the presenter asked other interesting things such as advice I'd give to anybody else thinking of starting up a business in the current climate. I told listeners that they should go with their passion. Finally as the interview drew to a close the presenter gave a brilliant plug for my products. I beamed as she described my fruit bars and gave out my website details for all of her hundreds of thousands of listeners to hear. She was even kind enough to ask me live on air which shops stocked the fruit bars, their price and my favourite flavours and I rattled of retailer after retailer.

I loved the ethos of another particular programme on a national radio station because it was all about how to enjoy life, through healthy eating, career changes, and work/life balance. They always seemed to give good life advice based on recent news stories or real life listener experiences. This motivated me to write my story from another perspective. This time round, rather than focusing on the recession, I focused on how starting up my own business had changed my lifestyle for the better, giving me a better work/life balance. Because I understood the style of their radio programme, I was able to explain my very real experience in their language.

Changing style for a different programme: This time in my email I focused on the highs and lows of my experience from my emotional journal of being made redundant, being worried about the future then focusing on the positive. This was my real story but with aspects highlighted that their listeners would be interested in. This was in contrast to when I applied to speak on the business programmes and focused on the economic climate, the recession and the sheer nuts and bolts of starting a business in such a climate. My real story again, but with a different emphasis. The business radio programmes had a different audience.

Another interview I did was simply about being a woman in business. It was interesting how the different radio programmes were all interested in my story but from different perspectives. My story, different applications, different audience, different style, but the same one story.

I reached millions of listeners through featuring on both national and local radio, creating awareness for my brand. To this day, I am regularly invited to take part in radio programmes and really enjoy doing so.

CHAPTER 8

HOW TO GET YOUR PRODUCT OR BUSINESS ONTO TV

"BE THE ONE TO WATCH, INSTEAD OF THE ONE WATCHING"

HOW TO BE THE 'ONE TO WATCH' INSTEAD OF THE 'ONE WATCHING'

The luxury of advertising a brand, product or service on television has long been the preserve of the huge corporations with equally huge pockets. The steep monetary costs associated with television advertising put it way out of the reach of many start-up companies, entrepreneurs and small businesses. However, I am happy to report that you can secure television coverage for your brand, product or service with creativity and persistence.

GETTING IN FRONT OF THE CAMERAS

There are a number of business entertainment programmes on television that brave entrepreneurs can and do apply to take part in. Such appearances do not cost money so are great for a start-up company. What you do need to do, however, is make the time to apply and participate, and have the bravery to appear in front of thousands of viewers as well as developing a thick skin for whatever comments will follow during and after your appearance.

Fame can be both good and bad, but more often than not, the exposure your product, business or service will achieve when well executed is priceless.

The publicity gained as a result of appearing on TV can often be used long after the programme has finished. Any company that's ever appeared on television can upload the clips to their website as well as other social media for all to view long after the event has finished. Other companies will include the fact that their product has been on television in their publicity material or packaging: "'as seen on TV".

There are so many programmes on terrestrial and digital channels that represent a great opportunity for your products or services. Current affairs, lifestyle, news, business and general interest programmes to name a few. All of them are continuously searching for content that will stimulate, entertain and update their viewers so why not offer content based on you and your products and services? This will give your product or service direct coverage into people's homes, not just hundred but potentially thousands and millions - for free.

CHOOSE THE TYPE OF PROGRAMME THAT SUITS YOU

→ *General programmes – like with magazines and radio stations, there will be business, lifestyle and documentary programmes that you can appear on This could be a guest that is interviewed about their story, as a feature that has been pre-filmed, or as an expert that comments on a particular trend, gadget, therapy or phenomena.*

→ *The 'Panel' type of programme, where you are filmed in front of a panel of investors and given a time slot to describe your product idea or service in the hope that one of the panel members, , will give you cash to invest in your business. The benefits of this are that whether the panel members decide to invest in you or not (and many times they do not), you have shared your brilliant idea with the world.*

This can serve to give you more exposure and great PR. There are several 'Panel' type shows across the networks. Programmes that actively try to help entrepreneurs to get their products to market, whose producers pick a number of entrepreneurs who are keen to be sold in shops on the high street. The entrepreneurs are tracked and supported during their progress in reaching the supermarkets and given help by experts along the way. The audience at home goes through the contestants' highs and lows and is rooting for them along the way.

HOW TO APPLY TO BE ON TV

You can apply to be on these shows just by writing to the features editor of that programme (see the credits at the end of the show and jot down the names of the researchers).

All major TV channels have websites where you can find out which shows they are recruiting for. If you Google the channel followed by "Be on a show" you will arrive at the area of that channel's website that lists the programmes that are being recruited for and includes downloadable application forms. Be as interesting as possible with your applications.

Also Google and email the programme researchers. If your story is topical or fits in with a theme that they are pursuing, or can be linked to statistics that have been in the press lately then the likelihood of your being selected as a guest feature for the show increases significantly. Timeliness and relevance are key, as is having the boldness to apply.

Also websites such as 'Star Now' will keep you updated via weekly or daily emails as to which new shows are recruiting. You can subscribe to these emails for free. Some of the posts on Star Now are for members only, i.e. those who have paid a fee, but there are plenty of open applications for everyone to apply to.

YOU CAN CREATE YOUR OWN CHANNEL

If you don't like the thought of taking part in some of the programmes on television, why not create your own channel? Internet platforms such as YouTube allow ordinary people to create their own channels and upload their own content for free. This is an increasingly popular way forward for many entrepreneurs, start-up companies and businesses which are all using the internet to connect with their customers and target audiences. Some of these channels have hundreds of thousands of followers. Yours could, too.

TOP TIPS: GET ON TV

1. *Contact the features editor of the entertainment, business and factual programmes that your product or service is suitable for. You can find contact details at the end of each programme and also by conducting a search on the internet.*

2. *If you are interested in on a specific channel, do an internet with the words 'be on a show' with the channel in the search bar. That will generate a link to how to apply for the shows on that channel.*

3. *Sign up to the aspiring actor websites. These often advertise for ordinary people to take part in documentaries .If you sign up at the basic level this is free – see my website* **www.fruitful-business.com** *for list of websites that you can sign up to.*

4. *If you feel you are able to share your business experience or expertise, contact the features editors with an outline of your proposal. The more current, interesting or topical it is the better.*

5. *Create Your own TV channel on the internet. This is a way forward for several start-ups with some channels gaining hundreds of thousands of viewings.*

MY STORY

Having contacted several business and lifestyle television programmes and only having received standard bounce backs, my enthusiasm had started to wane. As an optimistic person, I generally have a sunny disposition, but what felt like the millionth standard response ("Due to the huge volume of emails we cannot reply to all") was starting to take the biscuit.

HOW I GOT MY FOOT IN THE DOOR

Rather than apply excitedly to everything as I did in the beginning, my applications became no less frequent in number but instead more automatic. The tone I wrote was the same enthusiastic tone as ever, because I'd perfected the emails at the beginning of the process when I was very enthusiastic indeed; however, the actual process of hitting send, amending the name of the addressee or the headline became a matter for the diary. I had diarised applications on my daily to do list. I saw sending them as something I needed to do that would one day, according to the law of averages, yield a result. I would often sit in front of the television with my laptop in the evening trying to firing off my daily quota of emails. Would my persistence ever pay off?

When my mobile rang one morning following one such evening, my heart began to beat uncontrollably when I heard the words, "It's Beverly from the BBC. Thank you for your email, is this a good time to talk?" Wow was it a good time to talk, never better: I wanted to leap down the phone and give Beverly a huge hug. I trembled with excitement, trying desperately to maintain a professional tone on the telephone while answering her questions. After what seemed like an eternity of interrogation regarding the facts and figures in my story and business, but in reality was probably only 20 minutes, Beverly finally said that if I was available next week she would like to send a film crew to my house and film me for two days.

HOW I PREPARED FOR THE SPOTLIGHT

I danced round the house, excitedly thanking God. I couldn't believe it. The adventure that I had been hoping for, working towards had begun. I soon stopped dancing as the stark reality of my children's handprints on the living room wall sank in. They're coming to my house to film... The BBC are coming to my house to film, yikes I need a painter, a decorator, a thoroughly good clean, never mind the living room, what about me I need a makeover! Gosh I need to lose a stone, I had less than a week to get everything done. And so my frenzy filled preparations began.

Thankfully my parents, who live down the road, had a person decorating their house. I leapt into the car, driving straight round to Mum and Dad's. Bursting through the door, I explained hastily that I needed to borrow their workman for a day, given the BBC's imminent arrival. Mum and Dad kindly agreed and with their nod, I ushered their decorator swiftly into the car and round to my house.

No sooner had the smell of fresh paint started to waft through the house when I realised the carpets would need restoration too, then I looked up at the blinds, alas. In fact imperfections that never normally bothered me now seemed larger than life. I then began to wonder whether the BBC would want to film in the kitchen too and what about the corridor? How on earth could I get it all done?

Thank God for my very good friends who kindly came round to help me in lick my house into shape. I had a couple of them in the kitchen rearranging things while the workman painted the living room. I nipped out to buy cleaning fluids and while driving back I looked at the time. Oh no, amidst all the excitement and commotion there was one person I forgot to tell; David, my husband. He would be arriving home soon from a business trip. I raced home but it was too late. David had walked into his house to find a strange workman painting and a group of ladies giggling in the kitchen.

I turned my attention to my own appearance. I hadn't seen the inside of my gym for a while but headed there early Saturday morning. A hastily booked session with a personal trainer left me a few centimetres trimmer and walking taller. I'd never sweated so much in the gym prior to that and never have I since.

The icing on the cake to my preparations came when I was discussing what I'd wear for the film. I would need two outfits, one for each day of filming, with the second day of filming to comprise a live interview in the studio.

As my sister couldn't accompany me at such short notice she suggested I made use of a personal shopper. This was new territory for me. I telephoned all of the large department stores to see if I could book an appointment for the Monday morning. I eventually found a personal shopper willing to fit me in on Tuesday, the day before I was due to be filmed. Talk about the 11th hour.

Makeover time: At the high-end department store I was greeted by a young trendy teenager wearing tiny shorts. I explained that I needed to be transformed into business guru extraordinaire in time for the BBC the next day and that I needed two outfits. The young lady was very confident, and said she knew just what I needed. I sat anxiously in the personal shopping suite while she went to look for outfits that were up to the task. I was curious as to what she would return with. My fears were quickly allayed when she came back with a number of exquisite pieces: colours I'd never considered wearing, but really stylish. I was soon leaving the checkout having purchased the lot including matching accessories.

So I was ready on Tuesday night, just. I went through my mental checklist. House sparkling – tick; clothes ready – tick; garden ready - tick. Yes my husband did give the front lawn a quick mow just in case the BBC wanted to film the outside. He felt it was a tad superfluous but mowed it to help ease my anxiety.

COPING WITH FILMING

After a sleepless night I awoke to the knock of the BBC at 6am. I needn't have worried so much. The cameraman and his crew were lovely, putting me at ease instantly with their polite comments about my home. I explained how it had taken a near heart attack and an army of friends to get it into that shape. We laughed and got down to the business of filming, which entirely focused on the kitchen.

I had never appreciated just exactly how much time filming a short piece can take. They wanted to film me giving my family breakfast. Breakfast that morning was pancakes and fresh fruit. I opened the oven and gave out the pancakes. I thought we would then move onto the next piece, however, they wanted to film me giving out the pancakes again but from a different angle, and then again and again. I was really surprised. It's a good job I had bought enough pancakes to feed an army. I think we spent about an hour on eating pancakes before they finally filmed me making my children's packed lunch boxes using my very own fruit bars. The cameramen were absolutely lovely: so creative professional and polite.

The final show that went out was brilliant for my both my business and products. I created awareness for my fruit bars in millions of homes. I was able to refer to my fruit bars 'As seen on the BBC' in both my publicity material as well as my pitches to the various retailers that I was targeting. Also, my appearance on the BBC set the ball rolling for further appearances as well as invitations to speak at conferences.

CHAPTER 9

HOW TO GET ONTO THE PODIUM

"PUT YOURSELF UP FOR AWARDS, IT'S THE TAKING PART THAT COUNTS"

IT'S THE TAKING PART THAT COUNTS

When you have a great product or service, your customers need to hear about it, What better way to tell the world about the wonderful virtues of your products or service than to be nominated for or win an award?

The brilliant thing about entering awards is that it doesn't matter whether you win them or not. Although winning is the desired outcome with awards, to be honest, it really is the taking part that counts. Simply making the shortlist, or being a runner-up has immense benefits, and the publicity you can generate for your product is very worthwhile indeed. If you are shortlisted for, or win an award, you can publicise this fact on your website, *Twitter, Facebook, LinkedIn* and a whole range of social media.

If you make the shortlist, even during the early rounds you will still feature in the publicity material generated by the award hosts, typically appearing in their printed brochures and on their website, and even on the day of the awards interested parties from your industry are likely to be present. By doing this you gain interest up front and your audience will be keen to see how you perform. The fact that you have been shortlisted from hundreds of other companies demonstrates that you are an up and coming force to be reckoned with, a company worth investing in, a brand worth watching.

ENTERING AWARDS MAKES SENSE
FOR SO MANY REASONS:

1. *Awards enhance your reputation. Winning an award can give a business or new start-up instant trust in the eyes of customers, future customers, and consumers. Everyone loves an award winner and wants to be associated with success.*

2. *Consumers choose award winning products and brands. For example, have you ever been in the supermarket trying to choose a wine or cheese to serve at your dinner party? Faced with two similar product choices and no prior experience of either product, but with one product clearly displaying an award, which one would you choose?*

3. *The same occurs when choosing restaurants, hotels, and other services. In the absence of prior knowledge, a good review or the display of an award symbol can influence a consumer's choice in favour of one establishment over another.*

4. *Awards enhance the credibility of your product, business or service by placing you at the top of the league alongside other leading or noteworthy players in your field.*

5. *Awards enhance your visibility through the coverage the awards receive and also the PR that you can generate from being associated with an award in the lead up to, during and long after the event.*

TYPES OF AWARD YOU CAN ENTER

There is a huge range of awards out there. In essence if you can make it or do it, there is probably an award out there that you can win. I'm going to name some of the types of awards here just to help you get started.

→ *Awards related to business stage, in other words, the length of time your business has been running. For example, you can find start-up awards for owners who've only been running between 0 and 12 months, 1 to 2 years then 2 years plus.*

→ *Awards based on your business size for example, small, medium and large, with turnover parameters defined for each one.*

→ *Business awards for each type of product or industry, whether that be food, services, environmental, educational, author based, construction, etc.*

→ *Awards based on person profile: Entrepreneur, Young entrepreneur, Mumpreneur, Oldtrepreneur.*

→ *Gender specific awards: Women in Business awards, for example.*

→ *Awards aimed at celebrating the achievements of people of a particular ethnicity, for example The Scottish Asian Business Awards.*

→ *Awards with a regional emphasis: The London Business Awards, the South East Business Awards, the Welsh Business Awards.*

There are award categories that you'll be able to find perfect for your product or service.

HOW TO FIND AWARDS

The easiest way to find awards to enter is by searching the internet for awards connected with your product and or industry. Put them in your diary so that when the time comes round to enter, you'll be ready and raring to go. Scheduling each award will give you a timetable to work towards in terms of collecting the necessary evidence to submit with your award applications as well as garnering the support of people who can give you testimonials and references to enhance your application or even nominate you for your desired award if required.

Finding awards the easy way: An even easier way to find awards to enter is to sign up to the newsletters produced by companies that specialise in collating information on awards. These companies specialising in award information list when an award is taking place, which industry, what the deadline is and so forth.

You can receive regular award updates, newsletters and bulletins sent regularly to your email inbox. The reason that these companies collate information on all of the awards that are taking place is because they would like you to use their award entry services. For example, if you would like to enter an award and you do not want to go through the effort of completing the application form yourself or you feel you need expert help in applying for the award, these companies will help you do apply for will charge you a fee. Depending on the type of award entered, this could run into the thousands of pounds. These companies boast high success rates in assisting people to both enter and win awards. They will typically have a phone conversation with you about your product or business and draft your award entry on the basis of the information that you have provided. They may even get you to fill out a form to answering questions which again they will re-draft into an award winning entry. But I believe that with a well thought through application you can have just as high a success rates as the experts.

There is no magic formula to winning awards but some key principles I've found the most helpful include these top tips:

TOP TIPS: BEING SHORTLISTED FOR AND WINNING AWARDS

➜ *Honesty, and succinct but colourful descriptions.*

➜ *A clear well thought through case that is a credit to you and your product.*

➜ *Inclusion of supporting evidence where possible, for example your website, any positive newspaper articles, testimonials, other awards you've won.*

➜ *If samples of your product are required, make sure they are the very best, freshest version of your product that you have access to and make sure you package them well to avoid damage in the post. That extra care and attention taken with the bubble wrap really can be the difference between your products arriving in pristine condition or damaged.*

➜ *Often awards require public votes to go through to the next round. If this is the case, then I recommend posting the awards link to all of your social media pages such as Facebook, Twitter, LinkedIn, and literally ask people on these forums to vote for you, your business or your company. This certainly makes a difference if it's a numbers game.*

➜ *Most award forms usually contain a section where you can describe any other reasons to support your application. I would definitely mention here whether you are supporting a charity with your particular product or service, and whether you will*

---

be benefitting the community in some way. For example, have you given a young person valuable work experience? Do you plan to do more as your organisation grows? Everything you write down on the application really can help, no matter how small a thing that you perceive it to be. It can make the difference, so add as much positive detail as you can think off.

AWARD DINNERS, CEREMONIES, EVENTS

Once you've entered an award, spent time on acquiring votes, and made the shortlist, you can start to look forward to attending the awards ceremony. Typically glamorous affairs, you now have something to look forward to. The anticipation of winning really is spine tingling. Seeing your name or your company name in the brochure on the night of the event is awesome and another good way to showcase your products or service to your industry, including potential stockists.

Awards ceremonies give you the chance to meet other people in your industry, network and exchange business cards. They are a chance to meet potential buyers for your product or service range too because buyers often get invited to awards ceremonies by the hosts so it's a brilliant way to meet them and to have your product highlighted in the best possible way.

HOW TO GENERATE GOOD PUBLICITY
AROUND WINNING AWARDS

You can generate great PR by entering awards in the lead-up to the award and for a long time after.

Local press have a ferocious appetite of the local press award stories. Be sure to inform them of your award progress from entry, through to shortlist and, fingers crossed, the win. Every stage is a cause for a story. The local press love award-based stories because they put their local town on the map, engender community support and create that upbeat positive angle in the midst of depressing reports of crime and injustice that blight their pages. It's never too early to start publicising your participation in awards even before being shortlisted or before even winning one.

Your first press story: "Local company/business-woman (insert your company/name here) enters nation-wide award. The whole of our town is rooting for them. Their company specialises in x, y or z or has invented a new way of doing x, y or z. Your votes could make a difference and you could help by going to x website. The results will be known on x date".

Such a feature goes nicely alongside a picture of you with your fingers crossed and, more importantly, your product.

Your second press story: relates to the fact that you've been shortlisted for the award, with headlines such as "Local company vying for number 1 position" or "Local businesswoman shortlisted for national awards", The story you create in this short listing phase is about how you beat hundreds to make the shortlist, how you've been thankful for local support and how you're hopeful of the prize.

FINALLY IT'S THE WINNING STORY:
"LOCAL BUSINESS SCOOPS TOP AWARD!!"

By reporting on each stage of the competition you have 'several bites of the cherry' with which to have an impact on the readers. Your product is kept in the press for several months and your product becomes well known. People will remember, "that's the brand that I read about in the paper, I'll try that, I'll support local", "The product must be good if it won or was shortlisted for an award" and so forth. Before long, you will be getting invitations to attend local business forums - great for networking - or speak at local schools, and this will keep the wheels of your PR machine well lubricated.

HOW TO MAKE YOUR AWARDS WORK FOR YOU

Once you have been shortlisted for or won an award, the organisers will give you a badge or logo of recognition endorsing your new prestigious status. You are entitled to use this badge/logo in various formats. For example, you can have stickers made to apply onto your products. You can post the logo in a prominent position on your website. You can also use it in press articles, as well as at the end of every email you send or communication you write giving yourself maximum exposure for the accolade of being shortlisted for a prestigious award. Other logos/badges given out often relate to finalist in such and such awards which is also a brilliant accolade to shout about. Whenever you enter an award, get shortlisted or reach the finals, it's time to tell the local press, update your website, tweet about it, notify friends and family on *Facebook*, include it in your *LinkedIn* status and any other social media that you use. This is your platform. Own it. You have worked hard to get this far.

HOW TO USE YOUR AWARD TO PITCH FOR CUSTOMERS

Your potential customers would love to know about any awards success you have had, whether you made the shortlist, were a finalist or a winner. This really sets you apart from competitor brands, businesses products and services. It is therefore important that you use your award accolades during any 'pitch' that you make when trying to acquire new business. This could be verbally, in meetings, or as part of your presentation pack or slides for formal meetings.

MY STORY

HOW I SCOOPED MULTIPLE AWARDS

When I decided to start my own business, one of the seminars I signed up for was entitled 'Why you should enter Awards'. I found the title interesting because prior to signing up for this I thought that awards were really for the big league companies to pat themselves on the back. I'd never perceived the benefits that could be achieved for my own start-up endeavour. As I wanted to do every single thing possible in my power to make my business succeed, I went along to this seminar enthusiastically hoping to learn something and learn I did.

The speaker at the awards seminar was a young chap, wearing jeans, a T-shirt. When he spoke about how he had launched his male grooming range of hair care products, mainly using awards to fuel his publicity campaign, my mind leapt into overdrive. In fact, winning his first award had helped him to convince a big UK supermarket chain to trial his products in their stores, even though most supermarket aisles in personal care were dominated by huge multinationals. In fact, so useful had his company found entering awards that they decided to employ an awards company to target all of the awards relevant to them and enter on their behalf on a full time basis.

I was sold. If they could place such importance on awards and even pay to have a company entering awards on their behalf then it must be well worth giving it a go. I left the auditorium buzzing with ideas. However, I didn't have the money to pay the 'awards entry' companies that I'd just found out existed. I was going to have a crack at applying for awards myself. And so I began, trawling the internet for any type of award that I could enter. New start up awards, regional awards, food specific awards, awards for entrepreneurs. I was quite awestruck as to how many different types of awards there were. That's why I'm confident that if you look hard enough, you're bound to find not just one award but several that you can enter for your own business, product or service, even if you've only been in operation for a short time, which was the case with my fruit bar company.

HOW I COMPLETED MY ENTRIES

Some of the awards I found required a large entry fee. I steered well clear of those. To my comfort, I found several that did not require an entry fee at all or just asked for a nominal amount to cover their admin charges. It was these that I got stuck into. The first hurdle was the length of the forms: seriously lengthy. I can understand how people might be put off applying for awards because of the level of detail required, but in my case, I felt that the time commitment was worth it. I had nothing to lose but everything to gain.

Access all areas! The forms were lengthy and questioned the ins and outs of everything; why I started the business, how many employees I had, what my motivations were, what my turnover was, what my financial projections were, chapter and verse of basically everything. Some of the sections of the award entry forms were a little alarming, for example the financial data requested. I found this daunting because being a start-up business I didn't have all of the numbers requested. Rather than be put off by financial data sections or leave blank space, I would explain that my business was in its infancy. In place of actual turnover for example, I would put down projected future turnover based on my plan of action.

I continued to apply for awards as my business grew and I did start to get great figures, for example a few months' worth of trading, I would project the figures forward with an asterisk and footnote explaining that they were projected figures based on the initial months plus an adjustment applied for growth rate, market trends, planned marketing activities and so forth. As long as I was honest on the application form with regard to my formula for coming up with my optimistic figures, I felt happy that, if challenged, I was transparent. I could sleep at night. I've always believed in business that is key.

I found the other sections of the forms easier to complete because I knew the answers to questions such as why I had started the business (i.e. being made redundant, pursuing my passion, wanting to make a difference by contributing to healthy eating with my natural fruit bars etc.)

Because I'd done my market research, I found it easy to list reasons on the entry forms as to why my fruit bars would succeed in the marketplace.

I conveyed my answers with such a passion that anyone reading my applications would stay awake.

As I entered more awards I became well versed at it. The section that typically appears on the application form, "Any further evidence in support of your application" became a joy to complete. I use the word became, because initially I didn't really know what to put here. My mind was blank. However, the more applications I filled out, the more confidence I gained. It became apparent that this section was truly a gift, because in this section I felt that I could be unique, individual and not be judged in the narrow confines of some of the other sections.

I decided to list anything virtuous that I believed and had achieved, any obstacles I'd overcome to get to where I was, any hopes I had for the future, how my business had made a difference to the community, and the lives of others.

For example, one of my objectives for my business was to support charity however, when I started the business, I was not making any profit at all. I was barely making a living. Despite this, from day one, I was determined that any business endeavour I was a part of should make a positive difference to the world. Even though I was a start-up, I felt that I could still do something. No matter how small I wanted to start how I meant to continue. I visualised my efforts for charity and humanity in the initial stages as a drop in the ocean, but a drop whose ripples would reverberate outwards until they finally reached somebody.

Making a difference: In the absence of profit, I decided to support a charity that helps small business communities in the developing African countries. I chose a charity that helped other women predominantly in Ghana to start their own community business projects with start-up capital. The charity that I decided to support ran sponsored walks, treks and events around the UK country to raise funds. Rather than give profit as I had none, I donated fruit bars to these events. The charity was so grateful because it meant they could provide their walkers and volunteers with yummy natural energy giving fruit bars. This would in turn help them to complete their walks, and all for free. Just my own small way of helping.

It was this type of information I shared in the section of the forms entitled "Any further evidence in support of your entry" I pasted and copied sections of my chosen charity's website which showed that my company was an official sponsor.

Other forms of supporting evidence I added to my entries included my community work. As an avid believer in community, I often helped out in local schools by giving business talks to students using real life examples from how I built my product range. In support for my entries, I pasted in the positive feedback that I had received from schools.

HOW PRACTICE MADE IT EASIER

As I continued to make applications, the process became easier and the process less daunting. Some of the awards asked the same types of question so found that I could look to previous forms I'd filled out for inspiration and improve on them each time.

MY FIRST TASTE OF VICTORY

The first award that I won was of one of the prestigious in my industry: considering the awarding body only gave out 12 awards that year, a pretty special accolade indeed. The awards were 'The Oscars' of the food industry and attended by over 2000 people, with the prize-giving ceremony taking place at a glitzy London venue. Entering these awards felt like a modern day David vs. Goliath battle with many of the recipients of these awards being industry giants such as Tesco and Unilever. Emerging with a winning accolade was a real tearjerker for me and a testament to the fact that you really can go head to head with the big guys and win. There's nothing I can say to quite describe it. To top it all, of all the people that I could have ended up sitting with at the awards ceremony I was next to a senior person from a major retailer: the very same company I'd been trying get hold of for months!

My fervent efforts in staying up all night making award applications began to pay off and short listings started to roll including accolades from various award bodies for: Winner of Best Business of the Year, Winner for a Leading Industry Award, Finalist for a major banks business award, Finalist in a Future Brand Award, Highly Commended in a Food Award and so on. All of these awards were brilliant for self-esteem and motivation in my uphill journey. Each award was like an oasis in the desert, a real boost in tough times and, of course, in the business sense, a benefit in terms of publicity for the brand and company presence.

My awards helped me to gain favourable PR for my business and products in the media, opened doors for me and also strengthened my pitch to potential customers.

CHAPTER 10

HOW TO REACH THE MASSES

HOW TO REACH THE MASSES WITH YOUR PRODUCTS AND SERVICES

You have a wonderful product or service that you know people will love. Wouldn't it be great if you could reach as many people as possible with it? You certainly deserve to, after all the effort you've put in so far. The good news is that there are many routes to reach the masses.

Many of you will already be planning to sell your products and services to your customers 'face to face': from your home, at special events, a kiosk or space you've rented or bought, perhaps a stall, door to door and so forth. I come across many business start-ups who use this face-to-face approach, which can be very satisfying and rewarding providing direct 'face to face' contact with customers.

However, selling your products and services on your own may limit your potential, because face-to-face sales are dependent on the number of people with whom you are physically able to come into contact. Face-to-face selling also requires you or your representative to be physically present to facilitate a sale every time, so limits you when you are sick, on holiday, resting and pursuing other matters.

While face-to-face is a good start, if reaching the masses is your goal, in addition to what you can achieve face-to-face, you will need to consider other options to help you to reach a significantly wider audience and boost your growth potential.

Reaching the masses involves 1) significantly increasing your production quantities, and 2) increasing your reach, for example by utilising a range of distribution channels.

HOW TO REACH THE MASSES:
INCREASE YOUR PRODUCTION

The method you choose to increase your production will depend on what goods and services you are selling. For example you could:

1. *Consider employing people to help you produce more of your items. This needn't be as overwhelming as it sounds. By appointing freelancers or students you can maintain flexibility.*

2. *Consider acquiring equipment. A baker I knew wanted to take her business to the next level. To increase her quantities, she acquired some industrial mixing equipment from an auction and rapidly upscaled her production capabilities.*

3. *Approach a manufacturer to produce your product range or brand on your behalf. The benefits of this are that you don't have to purchase any equipment or hire premises. There are plenty of 'win-wins', as the manufacturer may have spare capacity, and producing your goods in addition to their own will create economies of scale for them.*

4. *If you are a practitioner, you could develop a process and license it, so that every time other practitioners use your process you command a fee.*

5. *Create products (training materials, DVDs, webinars, books, CDs) from the knowledge you have of your craft and distribute these.*

HOW TO REACH THE MASSES: INCREASE YOUR REACH

Increase your reach by enlisting others to sell your goods and services. These might include wholesalers, retailers, retail chains, other outlets, online stores and so forth. Identify the types of outlet with which you feel your products and services have a good fit. You will need to contact these in order to arrange appointments to show your products or services.

> *Why enlist others?* Enlisting other outlets will help your business become scalable and improve your growth potential, as described in Chapter Two.

WHOLESALERS

Wholesalers purchase large quantities of goods to sell on to a wide range of retail outlets nationwide. The benefit of using wholesalers is that they will widen your distribution significantly without you having to approach hundreds of individual independent stores. They already have the contacts and the distribution in place too to reach the masses. They are also a destination for hundreds of retailers.

RETAIL CHAINS AND SUPERMARKETS

As a nation, we purchase over 97% of our groceries from the major multiple supermarkets. That's a serious amount of goods. Being stocked on the shelves of the supermarkets gives you access to consumers nationwide. You do not have to be present when a consumer picks up your products from a supermarket shelf, and many are open 24 hours a day.

DISTRIBUTION ONLINE

The internet provides you with a shop window to the world. You may already have your own website or be planning to build one, which is great. However, to use this global shop window well, it's worth having your products and services displayed on other websites too, especially websites and online stores that will take orders for your products and despatch them on your behalf. That frees you up so that you are not continuously dealing with postage and packaging.

HOW TO CONTACT WHOLESALERS, RETAIL CHAINS AND ONLINE DISTRIBUTORS

It can sometimes be tricky to get hold of buyers. When you phone a large organisation and ask to speak to the buyer of socks, or the buyer of bananas, the receptionist will often refuse to put you through to them unless you have the specific name of the person with whom you'd like to speak.

Although this can be frustrating, don't get angry with the receptionists: this is often corporate policy and the receptionists are performing their role of 'gate-keeper'. They do this because buyers are incredibly busy, and often get bombarded with dozens of cold calls. However, don't let that deter you, because getting an appointment with the right person to show your products to is key to getting them listed by these outlets.

HOW DO I GET PAST THE 'GATE KEEPERS' AT RECEPTION?

The head office contact details of retail chains, supermarkets, shops and wholesalers are readily available on the internet and in trade directories and catalogues found in the larger libraries. These sources list high level contacts, for example directors, accounts, customer services, etc.

While the contacts listed may not necessarily be the people responsible for buying your goods or services, they are a good place to start in terms of getting the name of the right person within the organisation. You can always email or phone these 'high' level contacts with your enquiry. More often than not, when you contact them, they will be able to look up their list of internal contacts and give you the name of the actual person you need to direct your enquiry to, or indeed forward your query on to the right person. Armed with the correct contact details, you will no longer be stuck at reception.

PERSISTENCE PAYS OFF

When contacting these large outlets, sometimes you will be passed from pillar to post, with each person naming someone else as the person you need to speak to. Grit your teeth and bear it until you come to the right name. It often helps if you mention the last person who gave you their details, i.e. "Mr X or Mr Y told me you're the best person I need to speak with about". This way, you have a credible inroad to their attention, as they don't want you going back to Mr X or Mr Y to complain that they were unhelpful.

Once you do get the right name and contact details, you need to secure a meeting, because it's always best to present your goods in person rather than sending them in by post. In person, you can communicate with passion and respond to any queries the buyer may have.

Securing a meeting can be a challenge. Because buyers are incredibly busy, they won't always reply to your calls or emails. Don't take this personally: instead, keep trying with your phone calls and vary the times of day.

With your emails, keep your approaches interesting and eye catching. For example, If you're the purveyor of fine scarves, rather than putting 'scarves' as the subject line in your email, why not use your knowledge of the market or recent events. This could be, 'New craze means scarves set for a record year!' A buyer of scarves is more likely to open that email, so as not to be behind on any new craze.

OTHER WAYS TO GET NAMES

In addition to the internet, catalogues and directories, you can get both names and introductions through networking face-to-face and online. When you go to events with other people in your field, why not ask those you meet for the names of the buyers you are trying to target? People are often ready to share those names with you and will look to you to reciprocate. Name swapping is pretty common.

TRADE FAIRS

Buyers from retail chains, supermarkets, wholesalers and independent shops often attend trade fairs looking for new products and new suppliers. Your products could be just what they're looking for. Renting a kiosk during a trade fair in your industry is great way to bring you into contact with people that want to buy and distribute your goods. Because trade fairs are not generally open to the public, attendees are normally industry professionals, so any interest you generate from trade fairs are likely to be significant.

It can be expensive to hire a large kiosk or stand at a trade fair, so perhaps you could co-hire space with another entrepreneur to keep costs down. Also, you could hire a smaller space but make it stand out with your marketing materials. Be sure to study the plans of the trade fairs before purchasing your space, to ensure that you select a plot in the line of visiting traffic and not tucked away or out on a limb.

Start visiting trade fairs now in order to familiarise yourself, so that when you are ready to launch, you make the best of your opportunity.

If your products or services are destined for the export market, check out the policy of the government department responsible for trade. They often provide substantial financial assistance for you to exhibit at international trade fairs, so check which schemes are operating if you feel that this is an avenue for you.

MEET THE BUYER EVENTS

Some retailers have 'meet the buyer' events where you can take your wares and have a brief introduction to the buyer responsible for your goods or service. Check out whether your target retailer has these and plan ahead to attend.

HOW TO PREPARE FOR YOUR MEETING WITH BUYERS

Your persistence has paid off, and you've now succeeded in getting appointments with the buyers in your industry. First impressions count, and with a busy buyer, if they are not impressed the first time round then it's unlikely that you'll be given a second meeting. So advance preparation for your meeting is key.

Arrange your presentation well. This could be in the form of slides, or hand-outs, or whatever materials you are most comfortable with. Start with some background about you, your company, your aspirations and growth plans for your products and services.

Regarding your products and services, let the buyer know:

→ *What your product and services are and their unique selling points.*

→ *Which type of consumer they are aimed at (male, female, age range, social, demographic).*

→ *Why your products are suited to that buyer's outlet or store, and the benefits to the buyer and his consumers of stocking your range.*

➙ *Product and pricing information.*

➙ *Any press coverage garnered, awards you've won, social media campaigns you are undertaking, and any promotional activity you have planned.*

When you leave the meeting, leave the buyer with a hard copy of your presentation, so that they can mull over everything that's been discussed in your absence. Always ask for next steps and how you can work towards getting your products listed in store. Sometimes you will need several meetings with the same buyer before they commit to listing your products. In between those meetings you may be asked to submit further information and product samples for their internal reviews, panels and discussions. Always submit your best and don't miss their deadlines.

THE DOMINO EFFECT

Once you get your products and services listed within a reputable outlet, others of their ilk tend to follow suit. This is because other retailers don't want to be seen as the behind the trends, so will often stock your products if their contemporaries have them listed. Customers of theirs facilitate this by saying to them, "when can I get product x in your store that I've seen elsewhere?"

Also the fact you are listed within a major player, or a major player's catalogue, is a signal to other retailers that there may be profits to be had from stocking your products or services, and they won't want to miss out. They are more confident about stocking your products because another retailer/ catalogue has taken the risk already. So although it may take a great deal of persistence to get your first retailer, the persistence is worth it, because the others will soon follow.

MY STORY

When I started my natural fruit bar business, I knew I wanted my bars to be able to reach as many people as possible. I determined that, in order to reach the masses, my products would need to be present wherever people shopped. I discovered a startling statistic. Although there are hundreds of thousands of shops in the UK, over 97% of all grocery products are sold through the supermarket chains. In order to reach the masses with my food products as was my aim, I needed to get into the supermarkets.

→ *The number 1 supermarket chain in terms of size in the UK has 30% of food sales*

→ *The number 2 supermarket chain has approx. 17% of all food sales*

→ *The number 3 supermarket chain also has approx. 17% of all food sales*

→ *The number 4 supermarket chain has 12 %of all food sales*

Just by targeting a few of these stores, I realised that I could achieve nationwide distribution and significantly increase the chance of getting into all of the homes in Britain.

IMPRESSING THE RIGHT PERSON WAS KEY TO MY GROWTH PLANS

It was essential that I gained appointments with the right person within each supermarket chain. I knew that each supermarket chain typically had just one main buyer per product category or product group. So, for example, the number 1 supermarket chain in Britain has approximately 2000 stores across the country. At its head office, there is one buyer who makes the decision on which fruit bars to stock across the country in all of its stores. If I could convince that one buyer to stock my brand of fruit bars and they agreed, as a result of that one person's decision, I would have access to 2000 stores spread across the country.

As all of the major supermarkets tend to operate in a similar way per product category, to get access to the whole of the UK via the supermarket chains, I needed to target and convince the head office buyers of the merits of my products.

PERSISTENCE PAYS OFF

The main difficulty I had was that supermarket buyers were so busy and inundated with requests for meetings from people wanting to sell to them. I had to be very persistent indeed to make it through the door.

I'd invested a huge amount of time in researching my market through focus groups and questionnaires and ploughed all my knowledge back into my product development. I'd visited hundreds of stores to learn as much as I could about what works. I'd spent time developing a brand and packaging that really captivated the target audience. I decided that the prize of mass distribution was worth all my effort given all the steps I'd taken to produce my brand of fruit bars.

After all the attention to detail, I was certain that my efforts were good enough to get onto the shelves supermarkets. After all, my product was now just as professional looking as the other products that had made it onto the shelves. In fact, my design company had done such a brilliant job with my feedback that we had an even better product than those on the shelves. I now needed to convince the head buyers at the supermarket offices why my products should be on their shelves.

HOW I DID IT

In the past when I'd worked for big corporate companies on behalf of their equally big brands, getting appointments with the supermarkets had been easy. Now I was on my own, a new brand that almost no one outside my own business networks and focus groups had yet heard of. How would I attract their attention?

After surfing the internet for head office contact numbers for each of the major supermarkets that I wanted to target, I began to telephone their switchboards. Because I didn't have the name of the relevant buyer for fruit bars, I was a little stuck when it came to who to ask for. A number of head offices were quite strict and told me they were not allowed to give out the name of a buyer. If I didn't know their name then they wouldn't put me through: it was as simple as that. I therefore had to use a series of detective-style techniques to begin to elicit the names that had been withheld from me.

The most successful was the technique I call 'Pick a name, any name' in which I would do one or all of the following.

Pick a name, any name: I sought out the trade directories in the business section of a large reference library. These listed the addresses, phone numbers and names for each retailer. The names listed typically related to high level contacts such as managing directors, senior trading people, etc. For me, I felt the higher up the better. I would then construct a polite email to that person asking whom I should contact in relation to my exciting new product. Their secretary would reply with a name or at least a department to contact. I found this to be a particularly useful approach because CEO's and high level people will always push the work downstream and have staff to do their bidding. I could then mention in my email to the name that I had been given that their CEO gave me their contact details. When it was a particularly high-level person, they were more inclined to respond to me.

And so I got the names of the buyers that I needed to speak to and arrange appointments with.

OTHER METHODS I EMPLOYED TO GET NAMES

When I struggled to get names for some of the key retail buyers, I asked other people at the events I attended. People at these events also asked me for any names that I had, too.

TRADE FAIRS

I attended trade fairs in order to showcase my products and connect with potential buyers for my products. Although I selected small stands to keep costs down, by studying the floor plans of the trade fairs in advance of purchase, I ensured that my locations within the trade fairs were in prominent locations. This paid off in terms of visitor numbers to my stand. At one of those trade fairs, I garnered the interest of the buying team for the second largest UK multiple supermarket chain, with whom I exchanged details and booked a meeting.

MEETING WITH THE BUYERS: MY PITCH

I prepared for my retailer meetings by putting together an informative presentation about my background, business and products. I used the knowledge that I'd gained from my focus groups, questionnaires, market trends, store visits and so forth to make my presentation relevant and interesting.

In particular, I covered information such as why my fruit bars were on trend, unique, who they were aimed at, why those people would buy them, pricing information, why the retailer was a good fit and so forth. I was careful to tailor my presentation to each retailer, using the knowledge that I'd gained about them from reports and store visits to demonstrate that I understood them and their environment.

I arranged this information into PowerPoint slides that I'd prepared on my laptop. Using my laptop meant that I could control the pace of my presentation, without the buyer skipping straight to the end.

I dressed my best and delivered my presentation with passion. At the end of each meeting, I gave the buyer a hard copy of the slides I'd presented on my laptop and asked regarding next steps. Sometimes these next steps involved a second and a third meeting. Other times, they passed me on to another department and the process of phoning, securing appointments, etc., started again.

VICTORY AT LAST

Within just six months of registering my business, I secured my first major retailer listing for my brand. It was one of the upmarket chains well renowned for their quality and customer service. The feeling I felt when they said yes was amazing. The thought of my fruit bars going nationwide, in a top chain! I couldn't beat that feeling.

Although they'd said yes, I still had several hoops to jump through before my products reached their shelves. For example, the retailer needed copious forms to be filled out, trading agreements to be signed, samples for their internal team to be provided, and more information about the factory manufacturing my products including quality standards certificates. They needed professional photographs to be taken of my products as well as a commitment to their delivery schedules.

The agreement with the upmarket retailer included trialling my fruit bars initially in 47 of their stores. They agreed that on the basis of this trial they would decide whether to extend my fruit bars to the rest of their 300 stores.

Much to my relief, my fruit bars performed exceptionally well at the trial stage, outselling the closest competitor product in the 47 trial stores by 2 to 1 within a matter of weeks. After three months, my fruit bars were rolled out to the rest of the stores within that retailer's portfolio.

THE DOMINO EFFECT

I took my success story to the other retailers that I was trying to get into. In my meetings with them, I discussed the rapid sales growth I'd encountered with the upmarket chain. This, I believe, gave them the confidence to give my fruit bars a try, too.

Soon I was in several of the major multiple retail chains. In addition to the major supermarkets, I also managed to get my fruit bars listed with major wholesalers, health shops and onto one of the largest online stores in the world. I was selling fruit bars while I slept!

AND SO TO THIS BOOK

Once I'd achieved success in my business, people started asking me if I would speak at their conferences, business events, on TV and on radio, which I did willingly because I believe that sharing knowledge can help people.

When I spoke, people had lots of questions about how they could start their own businesses too. They wanted to know everything I'd done. I often felt frustrated that I couldn't share much in a half hour speech, hence my decision to write this bare-all book. I hope that what I've shared will help you in your business journey.

CONCLUSION

I've written this book because I wanted to share my real life experience of starting a business with you. It's the kind of book that I wish I'd had access to when I started my business. In summary:

Chapter One describes how starting with the right mind set is key to your progress. Napoleon Hill reminds us that "life's battles don't always go to the stronger or faster man, but sooner or later the man who wins, is the one who thinks he can".

A business fuelled by passion is a force to be reckoned with. Chapter Two provides exercises to help you discover your true passion and explore ways to leverage your passion through your skill set. Chapter Two also shows how you can multiply your income potential way beyond the limitations of your physical presence through scalability.

Many of my personal business strategies shared within this book are actionable at low and zero-cost. For example, in Chapters Three, Four and Five, I show how you can gain essential knowledge to enhance your skills, understand your customers and market to develop products and services that people want to buy. All at zero cost.

Creating 'win-win' situations that benefit both parties is always a good way to do business, and several examples line the pages of this book. Chapter Six describes a particularly innovative 'win-win' solution which enabled me to enlist the services of a top brand design agency whose costs were way beyond my reach.

Having a fantastic product or service is a great achievement, but you need to let the world know about it. Chapters Seven, Eight and Nine help you to generate mass awareness of your products and services, reaching millions of people through television, radio the press and internet, all at zero cost.

Chapter Ten finally shows you how to get your products and services into the hands of the masses.

In writing this book, I have equipped you with ideas, methods and examples to help you to start your business.

THE TIME IS NOW

By sharing my experiences with you, I hope that you will draw from them, adapt, improve and make them relevant to your own situation. I'm not for one moment saying that my way is the only way. There are always new and better ways to do things, because the world is evolving and new resources are becoming available all the time.

New social media platforms are opening up all the time. Take advantage of them. The social media revolution has meant that as a start-up, you can publicise your business wider and faster for free.

Mobile apps and gadgets are becoming available that help you to perform previously time-consuming business tasks in record time. Make use of them.

The internet is a fount of free knowledge. Never before has there been so much information available at the click of a button for those who want to learn. Why not plug in?

Technology is making running a business easier. We live in a global village, where customers, staff and resources are just a click away. There are more opportunities to connect with people than ever before. Now really is a good time to start your business. So what are you waiting for?

KEEP IN TOUCH

I wish you every success in your business start-up and look forward to keeping in touch with you via my website **www.fruitful-business.com** As well as keeping in touch, on my website, you'll find links to the resources mentioned in this book which I will endeavour to keep up to date to help you stay ahead of the game.

16428616R00083

Made in the USA
Charleston, SC
20 December 2012